Christianity 101
Tracing Basic Beliefs

James W. White

WESTMINSTER
JOHN KNOX PRESS
LOUISVILLE · KENTUCKY

Book design by Sharon Adams
Cover design by Mark Abrams

First edition
Published by Westminster John Knox Press
Louisville, Kentucky

This book is printed on acid-free paper that meets the American National Standards Institute Z39.48 standard. ⊗

PRINTED IN THE UNITED STATES OF AMERICA

06 07 08 09 10 11 12 13 14 15 — 10 9 8 7 6 5 4 3 2 1

Library of Congress Cataloging-in-Publication Data

White, James W.
    Christianity 101 : tracing basic beliefs / James W. White.—1st ed.
        p. cm.
    Includes bibliographical references.
    ISBN-13: 978-0-664-22953-5 (alk. paper).
    ISBN-10: 0-664-22953-0
    1. Theology, Doctrinal—History. 2. Trinity—History of doctrines. I. Title: Christianity one hundred one. II. Title: Christianity one hundred and one. III. Title.

BT21.3.W45 2006
230—dc22
                                                                                2005042314

Contents

To Hayley and Lauren

Acknowledgments

I rage at my inability to express it all better.
You'd need to use both hands and cover hundreds of canvases.
                                        Claude Monet, to a friend

This book represents half a lifetime of work. I have loved doing it. It has been done in faithful company and pleasant environs.

It all began in Englewood, Colorado, when Linda Glenn (church librarian), Stuart Haskins (senior minister), and I did a "Basic Christianity" course for adults of First Plymouth Congregational Church. We used a notion of historical trajectory given me by Clarence Snelling of the Iliff School of Theology. Over the years, variations of this course were done at Moline, Illinois; Denver, Colorado; Westfield, New Jersey; and Colorado Springs, Colorado. Always folk seemed to like the learning and graciously offered suggestions for content and presentation.

In time the course moved toward a written form. Colleagues and friends read the drafts and made suggestions on how to say essential things better. Here's a list of principal lay readers who made wonderful contributions: Hays Alexander, Lucy Bell, Kay Branine, Janet Carpenter, Jim Diers, Steve Ferguson, Jerusha Goebel, Bruce Kuster, Virginia Lee, Linda Lemieux, Sharon Littrell, Eric Ridings, Debbie Saxon, John Saxon, Alan Severn, and Pam Shockley. I know I'm forgetting . . .

Many ministerial friends made helpful contributions, especially Benjamin Broadbent (UCC), Don Dunn (Catholic), John Hallsten (Lutheran), Jerry Trigg (Methodist), and Jan Valas (Czech Brethren).

Any number of excellent scholars have read drafts of the manuscript in process, most especially Roberta Bondi, Walter Brueggemann, and Justo

González, all in Atlanta. At Colorado College in the Religion Department, I've had counsel reads by Joe Pickle and David Weddle. Also, I'm grateful to Gil Bailie, Marcus Borg, and John Shelby Spong, who in passing through "The Springs," lecturing, gave me encouragement and ideas. Jon Berquist and Daniel Braden, editors nonpareil, have been supportive beyond measure.

I've been able to study and write in some wonderful locales, for example, the Tantur Institute in Jerusalem, the Abbey on the Island of Iona (Scotland), the University of Edinburgh, Yale Divinity School, and Columbia Theological Seminary in Decatur, Georgia. Several families have graciously provided retreat locations for writing: the Carris family for Breckenridge, Colorado; Scott and Lois Saunders for Arrowhead Ranch (near Fairplay, Colorado); and especially Jane and Bruce Warren for Taos, New Mexico.

Finally, I am grateful most of all to Patti Limpert White, person and wife extraordinaire.

For all, with their faith and gracious works, I hope I can remember Jesus' counsel to give thanks to God.

Thanks, God!

JAMES W. WHITE
COLORADO SPRINGS, COLORADO

Introduction

Since many have undertaken to set down an orderly account of the
events that have been fulfilled among us, just as they were handed
on to us by those who from the beginning were eyewitnesses and
servants of the word, I too decided . . . to write an orderly account
for you, most excellent Theophilus, so that you may know the truth
concerning the things about which you have been instructed.

Luke 1:1–4

Those whose vision cannot cover
  History's three thousand years,
Must in outer darkness hover,
  Live within the day's frontiers.
    Johann Goethe,
    Westöstlicher Diwan

We have this most interesting situation in the Christian religious world
today: there is a great deal of "spirituality" and little historical grounding
for most of it. In the nineteenth century, the reverse seems to have been
the case. Søren Kierkegaard complained that in Denmark, "there is no
lack of information in a Christian land; something else is lacking . . . ," and
what was lacking, he thought, was firsthand experience of the Holy. Today,
in all hemispheres of Christianity there are countless people who are spiritually enlivened but short on theological-historical perspective. Many, I
believe, would like to go deeper into their faith story. In this book I offer
Christian historical understanding to support Christian enthusiasms.

For more than twenty-five years I have taught a Christian groundings
course in churches, with the title "Introduction to Christianity" or "Basic

Christianity" or "BC 101" or—once, on request—as "Christianity for Dummies"! The class has been for inquirers, new members, believers who wanted to deepen their faith, confirmands, and professional colleagues. During all these years of teaching, I have looked for a suitable study book for the class that would incorporate *both* Bible *and* church history. No such single volume exists. To be sure, one can find a *Brief Outline of the Bible* and an *Overview of Church History*, but there is no single resource that is a biblical-church history "summary." This book comes close. Wholeness-of-faith-story is this book's first differentiating mark.

A second unique feature about *Christianity 101* is that each part covers four thousand years! In most religious histories the first chapters tell the early years of the faith—and that era's many aspects—and the end chapters recount recent time and aspects. Not so here. In these pages each of the four parts sweeps the entire story. So, if one were to read only one part (and it matters not which), the reader would "get a feel for the whole" of biblical and ecclesial (church) history. To read all the parts would be to gain an even stronger, holistic awareness—encountering some reinforcing repetition, of course. Each part, then, stands on its own, not in need of previous material in order to be understood.

Having indicated what this book is and how it proceeds, let me say what it is not. *Christianity 101* is not about how to become a Christian, what you are supposed to believe, or how to conduct your life. There are numerous books on such subjects. This book is, rather, about the significant events, people, and theology that have gone before us that make us who and what we are today. It is about how what now is Christianity came to be, at least in terms of basic belief. If it offers insight to grow in the faith, follow Jesus, understand doctrine, conduct your life, develop spiritually . . . well, that is an accompanying plus.

One of the challenges in organizing this volume has been to decide what topics to include. I have picked four, all basically related to what is central in our thought/beliefs/doctrine, or what might be considered "the true." Part 1 considers the central historical events that made Christians who and what we are. The reader may find it worthwhile to read this first, but, again, one could start elsewhere. Part 2 concerns itself with our basic theological understanding of God. Jesus is the focus of part 3, recalling our Lord in Older Testament ideas and persons, as well as in postresurrection understandings. The final part, dealing with the Holy Spirit, traces faith's insights through the millennia into the workings of the third member of the Trinity.

Each part is divided internally by three chapters having to do with biblical times, the early church, and the later church. Within these are sub-category time periods, to wit:

Premonarchic Millennium (2000–1000 BCE)
Time of the Kings and the Prophets (1000–550 BCE)
Second Temple Period (550–20 BCE)
Newer Testament Times (20 BCE–110 CE)
Struggling Centuries of the Church (110–500 CE)
The Age of Monasticism (500–1100 CE)
High Christendom Years (1100–1450 CE)
Reformations/New Worlds Era (1450–1650 CE)
The Ecumenical Age (1650 CE–Present)

The reader or a study group may want to take one, two, or three of these eras alone for consideration and conversation.

Some of this book's character is suggested in the above listing of eras. For one thing, BCE (Before the Common Era) and CE (Common Era) are used throughout, rather than the older abbreviations, BC (Before Christ) and AD (*anno Domini*). The main divisions of the Bible are presented as the Old*er* Testament and New*er* Testament so that we consider their difference primarily in terms of when they were composed, without implying that the earlier testament is somehow superceded. Throughout this volume, gender-inclusive language is used, with some help on this— at least, for "humans"—found by using the New Revised Standard Version of the Bible. I try not to let God be only masculine.

At the end of each part are some questions for consideration. These are offered both to help stimulate conversation and to make the historical material relevant to the present. Little in our dynamic faith is finally settled, so these questions can help open up what new thing God is doing. Or, to use a thought from radio comedienne Gracie Allen: "Never place a period where God has placed a comma."

As to the author's place in the Christian spectrum, I am an ecumenical mainline Protestant greatly influenced by "big tent" Catholicism. My specific denominational background is in the Christian Church (Disciples of Christ) early in my life, and the United Church of Christ (Congregational branch) most of my ministry. I am not unappreciative of conservative evangelical and pentecostal Christians, but the language, worldview, and passions of these sisters and brothers are not natural to me. Eastern Orthodoxy, the second largest Christian family in the world, is remembered as we go along but not traced as fully as Western development. The historical time line here runs mostly east to west (Middle East, to western Europe, to North America), more than northward into Russia or to the southern hemisphere countries or the Orient; but those compass paths all are touched upon.

Sad to report, religious history is given short shrift on the contemporary scene. Go to a Christian bookstore, and typically you will *not* find a "Church History" section. There will be shelves of Bibles and Bible commentaries and rows and rows of self-help books on prayer, family life, church management, and so forth—plus Christian rock DVDs and Jesus T-shirts!—but almost nothing that looks like the Christian story. I had a grandfather a little like that. He was born in 1881 and knew his Bible well, but of the time between when the Newer Testament canon closed and his own lived history began, he knew almost nothing! If that is our condition, it is a shame, because we have been enormously influenced by what has happened in the last 2000 years. If this book does no more than fill in some of the gap between Bible time and our own, it will have served a helpful purpose.

I hope, though, that it will do more, that it will be a resource bringing four thousand years of development into appreciation and grounding influence. Thus we might be kept from being "tossed to and fro and blown about by every wind of doctrine, [and] by people's trickery" (Ephesians 4:14). It should be most helpful to individual readers (Christians, inquirers, "church alumni," others) and as a teaching-learning text in adult religious education classes.

In addition, I hope this book can be a resource to pastors. Most seminary-trained clergy could, with a little recollection, do a rough outline of any one of the book's parts. I hope my having done it here might be helpful to clergy in teaching and preaching, perhaps saving a little time looking for sources.

The parts present our faith's long history as relevant trajectories. If presented well enough, people can understand them and carry them forward more faithfully. A list of "next step" or "going deeper" resources for each part is included in the "For Further Reading" section at the back of the book. Also there is a glossary of terms frequently used. As helpful as anything may be the time line at the end of part 1 (pp. 31–38).

Let us begin with the excellent words of the Protestant Reformer John Calvin:

> Is this what believing means—to understand nothing, provided only that you submit your feelings obediently to the Church? Faith rests not on ignorance, but on knowledge. We do not obtain salvation

either because we are prepared to embrace as true whatever the Church has prescribed, or because we turn over to it the task of inquiry and knowing. . . . It would be the height of absurdity to label ignorance tempered by humility "faith." (*Institutes of the Christian Religion*, 3.2.2–3)

Part 1

Central Historical Events

For ask now about former ages, long before your own, ever since the day that God created human beings on the earth; ask from one end of heaven to the other: has anything so great as this ever happened or has its like ever been heard of?

Deuteronomy 4:32

"Big Doors Swing on Little Hinges"
Source uncertain but illustrated by Blaise Pascal's quip in his *Pensées*: "Had Cleopatra's nose been a half inch shorter, the history of the world would have turned out differently."

In life there are critical moments that make all the difference: the birth of a child, a promotion, a move, an injury, a conversation, the death of a loved one. Such moments make previous personal history meaningful, give new self-understanding in the present, and point one forward. Similarly, a local church may recall turning times in its story: the call of a particular pastor, a destructive fire, a decision about an issue. Looking back, people of faith are inclined to believe, "The hand of God was somehow in the occurrence." In faith we say it is so. Theologian H. Richard Niebuhr puts it this way: "Responsibility affirms—God is acting in all actions upon you. So respond to all actions upon you as to respond to God's actions."[1]

In the four-thousand-year history of Christianity, there have been grace-filled moments, threatening occasions, formidable challenges, and little incidents that are remembered in collective memory as determinative. As in personal histories, these events interpret (a) prior happenings, (b) later developments, (c) the present moment, and (d) the future yet to be. In part 1 of this book, I want to indicate a number of

1

shaping events—some primarily symbolic—in Christian history, high-lighting ten that are absolutely central:

1. The exodus
2. Establishing Jerusalem and the temple
3. The exile (and return)
4. The resurrection of Christ Jesus
5. An edict of toleration
6. Incursions on the empire(s)
7. The posting of 95 debate theses
8. The discovery of the New World
9. An apple falls—the rise of science

and, perhaps, for our own time,

10. Vatican II

These ten serve as markers to help Christians remember basic occur-rences that still influence us. (The first three, of course, are shared with rabbinic Judaism.) I pick these because they have so very much going into them, they stand out in their time, and much flowed from them. In addi-tion to the ten, there are other important happenings in our faith story that help fill out the moving picture of where we have come from, what we value, and what we aim toward.

In these three chapters of the book, lower case bold type indicates the **significant happenings** and bold capital letters indicate **CRITICAL EVENTS**. As we move toward the telling, words already used in this text, words such as *exodus, resurrection,* and *Vatican,* probably need expla-nation. Definitions will be provided as we get into these events, but the reader may go directly to the glossary at the end of the book.

Now, to consider our faith's central historical **happenings/ EVENTS.** . . .

Chapter One

Biblical Times

Premonarchic Millennium (2000–1000 BCE)

(. . . but, first, a little note: Piously, the story of Christian faith begins with the creation of the world, generally, and of men and women, in particular. Such is true from the way the Bible is laid out, but there is a problem starting with scriptural chronology: the Genesis understanding of God/world/humanity is a relatively late development. It is introduced into Scripture only a few hundred years before Christ. In truth, our faith has been focused not so much on cosmology and origin of the species as on lived human history. So this chapter begins within a specific people's time.)

"Our faith," I like to say, "began around a campfire." Biblical scholars of a previous generation thought this may have been the actual case. The dramatic picture is of the tribes of ancient Israel gathering periodically, as gathered the tribes of ancient Greece or of, say, the Sioux nation in America. Nomadic people gathered for purposes of commerce, socializing, information-sharing, celebration, and more, including *storytelling*. One of the stories we can believe they told is that of escape from slavery in Egypt. We call it **THE EXODUS EVENT**.

The exodus is placed in memory around 1250 BCE. It is told in the Bible's book of Exodus (see, especially, chapter 14) and is spoken of over and over again in the Bible. Psalm 105, verses 1 and 37, is a wonderful poetic recounting of it:

> O give thanks to the LORD, call on his name,
>   make known his deeds among the peoples.

3

[Yahweh] brought Israel out with silver and gold,
    and there was no one among their tribes who stumbled.

The best prose capsule summary is Deuteronomy 26:5–9:

> A wandering Aramean was my ancestor; he went down into Egypt and lived there as an alien, few in number, and there he became a great nation, mighty and populous. When the Egyptians treated us harshly and afflicted us, by imposing hard labor on us, we cried to the LORD, the God of our ancestors; the LORD heard our voice and saw our affliction, our toil, and our oppression. The LORD brought us out of Egypt with a mighty hand and an outstretched arm, with a terrifying display of power, and with signs and wonders; and he brought us into this place and gave us this land, a land flowing with milk and honey.

The memorable escape may have happened for only a relatively small band of folk. It was a little hinge on which a great door (two world religions) swung. It has been immensely important for self-understanding to billions of the faithful in subsequent history.[1] The Israelites experiencing escape shared their dramatic story when they came together with others at regional shrines in Canaan. Over time, telling and retelling the story, kinsfolk came to "own it" as *their* story as well, much as people in the United States own a colonial era incident involving only a few—the Pilgrims' first thanksgiving.

Because of the exodus event, Israel looks back to make sense of its more distant past, adopting and recasting stories and legends of the tribes' ancient patriarchs and matriarchs, such as those of Abraham and Sarah. From Genesis 12, one can read of these foreparents' **move to a land that God would show them.** They moved from Haran (in today's northern Iraq) into "the promised land" (Palestine). They went "by faith." Abraham and Sarah's time was, perhaps, 1800 years BCE. The story line in Genesis, involving other patriarchs and matriarchs, is that our tribal ancestors landed in Egypt around the year 1700 BCE, going there for food in a time of famine. In Egypt they stayed for five hundred years.

That is how *they*—let me say *we*—got there, remembering that Christians share this story with Jews.

So, here they/we were in Egypt when God, faith affirms, led us out of bondage. It was a time of creation—indeed, *the* creation, the creation of a people. The story of exodus exercises commanding theological importance, for, "by *God's* grace, we were delivered from bondage and formed."

In the language of the Christian Newer Testament, the meaning of this event is that "once you were not a people, but now you are God's people" (1 Peter 2:10). Once we were without shape and void, but now we have found identity in the world and to ourselves.

When they assembled the Older Testament—after 500 BCE—the people of Israel would ask more about the origin of the world and of humankind. This creation they also attributed to God, but it is of secondary significance. Older Testament scholar B. Davie Napier put it this way to his students: "The Israelites reasoned that if God could create us, who were no people, into a people, then it would be a 'snap' to create the world!"[2]

We read history backward.

And forward.

In conjunction with the exodus, there occurs another happening of long-term significance: a **covenant is made at Mount Sinai**. This was a drawing together of the people with God into a lively community of mutual faithfulness. At the heart of the covenant was the Decalogue, otherwise known as the Ten Commandments. On stone it is put down how the people of Israel will relate to God and to each other. Most Western people today can recite one or two of the Ten Commandments. For many, the Commandments are bigger than the exodus.

In light of the exodus and the covenant, our story moves forward some more. Now **taking the promised land** of Canaan may be considered. The Israelites both occupied and conquered the land: "occupied" it by being there (some never left for Egypt) and "conquered" it by arms in combat. It takes several hundred years to really be ensconced but, year by year, the Israelites became the dominant presence in the hill country from Dan (in the north) to Beer-sheba (in the south). Consult a map of ancient Palestine-Canaan in the back of a Bible to get a sense of the land.

The winning of the land is attributed to the efforts of men and women called judges. During their time, 1200–1000 BCE, there was no king in Israel (Judg. 21:25). That was soon to change.

Time of the Kings and the Prophets (1000–550 BCE)

While the Israelites were taking over the hill country of Judah and Ephraim, their neighbors on the coast, the Philistines, were becoming threateningly expansive and increasingly successful in battle against the Israelites' loose tribal federation. More and more the Israelites looked for stronger leadership. They sought a king. First, by the prophet Samuel's anointing, they had a king named Saul. Later, a young captain named

David emerged as their most effective leader and was, also by Samuel, made king.

What David did during his forty years on the throne was to create a united kingdom. He drew the twelve tribes together into a oneness not previously known. In part he did this with a new-to-all-the-tribes capital city. The **ESTABLISHMENT OF JERUSALEM** with its **TEMPLE** (built by David's son, Solomon) must be read as a central event for all our subsequent Jewish, Christian, and Muslim history. City-with-temple became the home base, emotional center, and everlasting symbol of sacred space. Today people perceive Zion (Jerusalem) with its Muslim Dome of the Rock, its Church of the Sepulcher for Christians, and its Jewish Western Wall to be a "thin place" in the world where God and humanity draw close.

In addition to building the temple in Jerusalem and keeping the tribes together, Solomon was able to expand the borders of this emerging new nation. According to the Bible account, the country's borders went west to the Mediterranean, east to the Arabian Desert, north to Damascus (Syria), and south to an arm of the Red Sea. Looking back, we see the tenth century BCE was the geographical high-water mark of ancient Israel.

Unity of the tribes, however, did not hold.

After Solomon died in 926 BCE, the kingdom divided in two, as follows:

Location	Name	Capital	Composition
North	Israel – House of Omri	Samaria	10 Tribes
South	Judah – House of David	Jerusalem	2 Tribes

Though divided, the two kingdoms each held to faith in Yahweh, their God, as established by their ancestors. The northern kingdom, though, emphasized the "covenant with Moses" and worshipped in varied locations such as Shechem, Bethel, and Dan. The southern kingdom emphasized "covenant with David" and worshipped in Jerusalem only. King Josiah of Judah and the writers of the book of Deuteronomy (about 621 BCE) will contend that only kings who worship in Jerusalem can ever "do what is right in the eyes of the Lord."

During these centuries, a development of ethical importance for all subsequent history took place: **the voice of prophecy was heard.** Prophets of and for Yahweh arose. These were persons who appraised the moral, social-political-economic and religious life of the people. They delivered *the Word of the Lord* to kings and to the people. Prophets Amos and Micah, speaking in the north, called for justice and a renewed righteousness. The prophet Isaiah of Jerusalem joined them, speaking from the perspective of a radical monotheism. Though severe judgment was often the message, the prophets Hosea and Jeremiah also held out hope for forgiveness and restoration by God.

In spite of the best efforts of kings and prophets, these two little nations could not survive intrusion by the Middle East superpowers of the late eighth and early sixth centuries BCE. They succumbed. One of the important events for the history of the faith, therefore, has to be **the destruction of the ancient kingdoms** with subsequent **EXILE**. In 722 BCE the northern kingdom of Israel fell to the Assyrians. Then the residents were deported, creating for subsequent historical imagination "the ten lost tribes of Israel." Foreign populations were moved into the area, creating a mix of races with a jumble of religions. The southern kingdom held out for another 135 years, but in 586 BCE Jerusalem fell to the Babylonians. These invaders from the east razed the walls of the city, along with Solomon's temple. Judah's leading citizens were taken into exile, to live "by the waters of Babylon." There they dreamt of Jerusalem, which was no more.

We like to think that "central events" of life are the happy ones. That is not necessarily so, either individually or corporately, as the people of Yahwist (see glossary) faith discovered. The tragedy of the loss of city and temple was not forgotten. It remained a major event, sad and significant.

Tragedies, though, can create something new, something maybe better, though it may take a long time to decipher what the good is. With the northern and southern kingdoms conquered and their citizenry deported (much of it lost forever), there was a **scattering of Yahweh's people** throughout the known world. Such a scattering continued for centuries. It is called the Diaspora or "dispersion" of Israel. In time the people of the Diaspora reshaped the religion, enabling the faithful to learn that their religion need not be tied to a particular place or particular ritual practice observed in a particular building . . . and yet can live. Instead of making pilgrimages to Jerusalem and offering sacrifices in the temple there, our dispersed ancestors discovered alternative ways in faithfulness. They could go to synagogue, a local center for worship and learning, to pray and to study. They could study a collection of books that they called "the Law" and try, wherever they were, to walk in its ways. Here is how they speak of it in Psalm 119, verses 97, 103, and 105:

> Oh, how I love your law!
>   It is my meditation all day long.
> How sweet are your words to my taste,

sweeter than honey to my mouth!
Your word is a lamp to my feet
and a light to my path.

Eventually the law will be part of what we call the Bible.
Saying this, though, gets us a little ahead of our story.

Second Temple Period (550–20 BCE)

The exile in Babylon ended for the Hebrew people with a second exodus. In 538 BCE, after defeating the Babylonians, the victorious king of Persia told the captives from Jerusalem that their exile was over. They could **RETURN** home. Many did. Their return eventually resulted in these three important developments:

1. **Building a temple**—thus ushering in the Second Temple period
2. **Building a wall around the city**—thus providing greater political coherence
3. **Building the Bible**—thus fixing their or our first sacred text

Of these three, in the long run, the making of the Hebrew Bible is the most important.

The Torah or Law or Pentateuch (first five books of the Bible) as sacred Scripture came to "final form" in the century or so following return from exile. Next, the writing and oral sayings of the Prophets were, more and more, fixed. And thirdly, in the century just before Christ, the Writings (Psalms, Proverbs, etc.) came to be more or less sacred Scripture. By the year 90 CE, our ancestors put their arms around all three bodies of writing and called them by the acronym Tanakh:

T	- Torah	— Pentateuch
ana	- nebi'im	— Prophets
kh	- kethubim	— Writings

These texts, the rabbis decided by vote, would constitute the Bible or library of sacred writings essential to faith. They selected thirty-nine books, Genesis through Malachi, that became in the sixteenth century CE Protestant Christianity's Older Testament.

For people of the Diaspora, and for all Jews and Christians ever since, the Bible has been a resource of incalculable import. City-with-temple or no, our faith ancestors found the sacred scrolls/books to be sufficient for faith, instructive, comforting—and portable! The Bible could go anywhere! So it went—to Susa, to Alexandria, to Rome, to Kells, to Wartburg, to Boston, to the Sandwich Islands, and to Motel 6's. Doubtless it will be opened on third-millennium-CE interplanetary space flights. The faithful will read: "Shema/Hear, O Israel: The LORD our God is one LORD" (Deut. 6:4 RSV).

But let us return to the years BCE.

Persian rule over Palestine gave way in the late fourth century BCE to Greek control. Alexander the Great came conquering. His successors then established a Greek cultural presence that lasted for at least eight hundred years. A desecration of the Second Temple in Jerusalem by a Seleucid Greek king, though, happened. It **provoked a rebellion, the Maccabean revolt**. That revolt of the 160s BCE threw off Greek rule and gave the Hebrew people nearly a hundred years of relative political independence. It came to an end in 63 BCE, when the Romans captured Jerusalem. The Romans eventually appointed a non-Jerusalem Jew, Herod, called "The Great," to rule the area. In the years 19–20 BC Herod expanded, remodeled, and essentially rebuilt the temple, incorporating Roman architecture.

Newer Testament Times (20 BCE–110 CE)

It was probably under Herod's rule that **a child was born** to a woman named Mary in Bethlehem of Judea in the year 6, perhaps 4, BCE. The child, Jesus, grew up in Nazareth, a city in Galilee of northern Palestine. As an adult he became a wandering rabbi whose teachings were warmly received by many—and not so warmly by others. His teachings embroiled him in conflict with the religious leaders of his day and, ultimately, with Jewish and Roman political authorities. After a disturbance involving Jesus at the temple in Jerusalem, he was arrested and tried for blasphemy and sedition, found guilty, and executed on a cross as a common criminal. He died and was buried.

If this were the end of the story, no doubt we would know nothing of the man.

Something happened, though, that brought Jesus' life, teachings, and death into two thousand years of remembrance. That event was **THE RESURRECTION**. God raised him from the grave. God broke the bonds of death. This is the sine qua non in the development of Christian faith. On the third day after his death and burial, Jesus is seen again by his followers. They say, "He is risen!" Christ's resurrection changed them from dejected mourners to elated witnesses with a message of hope for the world. "He lives!" women and men proclaimed. The strong words of Paul in his letter to the church at Corinth say it best:

> Now I would remind you, brothers and sisters, of the good news that I proclaimed to you. . . . I handed on to you as of first importance what I in turn had received: that Christ died for our sins in accordance with the scriptures, and that he was buried, and that he was raised on the third day in accordance with the scriptures, and that he appeared to Cephas, then to the twelve. Then he appeared to more than five hundred brothers and sisters at one time, most of whom are still alive, though some have died. Then he appeared to James, then to all the apostles. Last of all, as to one untimely born, he appeared also to me. . . . But in fact Christ has been raised from the dead, the first fruits of those who have died. For since death came through a human being, the resurrection of the dead has also come through a human being; for as all die in Adam, so all will be made alive in Christ. (1 Cor. 15:1, 3–8, 20–22)

In light of the resurrection, other prior aspects to the life of Jesus gain importance. As suggested in the text by Paul just given, there is something important to be made of Christ's death. Paul comes to appreciate **the crucifixion of Jesus** as a means of reconciling humanity and God. The community of Christ—which becomes "the church"—will, more and more, come to affirm that "Christ died for us." Many interpretations of what that means will be made. Among them is one that suggests that Jesus is the "ultimate victim," who went to his death "blaming no one, forgiving all." By implication, if all are forgiven, there need be no more victims—ever.[3] Millions of victims later, this interpretation still awaits full acceptance and enactment.

Following from Christ's resurrection and, secondly, from dealing with his crucifixion, interest then grew in recapitulating Jesus' **teachings**, his **life and work**, and, finally, his **birth** story. Followers begin to comb through the Tanakh (the Older Testament) looking for clues as to the meaning of this man. They discover passages that seem to prefigure Jesus, such as "the suffering servant" passages of the book of Isaiah. The writer of the Gospel of John pushes the meaning of the coming of Christ as far back as one might go. He affirms that the divine essence, God's Word that was in the beginning, came to dwell in Jesus of Nazareth, thus making him "the anointed" of God, Christ, Messiah, the Lord, One with the Father God. John thus attributes cosmological dimension to this rabbi from the provinces!

Much more might be said about this Jesus, so absolutely essential to Christian faith. In fact, every part of this book does so speak, and the third part recounts his four-thousand-year(!) history. The point of these pages, though, is just that Jesus as the Christ is the centerpiece of our faith, made so by one event: his resurrection. For explication of Jesus' life, death, and resurrection we are indebted to **the Gospels** or "Good News" accounts **written by Matthew, Mark, Luke, and John.** Later generations of Christians spell out implications of the Gospels, such as the relationship of Jesus to and with God the Father, but with the whole of Jesus' life put together in the Gospels, he begins a future that yet beckons followers forward.

The book of the Acts of the Apostles, which follows the Gospels in the Newer Testament, speaks of another important happening in our faith history, namely, **the founding of Christ's church.** Fifty days after the Jewish festival of Passover is the day known as Pentecost. On that day, when the followers of Jesus were assembled for worship, the Spirit of God came upon them, "firing them up" to spread the good news of God's love through Christ in all the languages of all the peoples of the then-known world. See Acts 2:1–21 for this dramatic story.

The rest of the book of Acts is an account of the **missionary expansion of Christianity.** Acts suggests that the people of the Way made a three-step move: they went from (1) Jerusalem to (2) Judea and Samaria, and to (3) all the world (Acts 1:8b). The spread transpired, first, by Jesus' followers' making proclamation in the synagogues of the Diaspora. Soon, though, Christianity was attracting non-Jewish believers, "God-fearers," persons initially drawn to Judaism for its monotheism and ethics. They were further attracted when the Christian message of God's loving acceptance of all through Christ was proclaimed. So the church became more and more a Gentile (i.e., Greek) institution spreading throughout the Roman Empire. The story of Christianity's growth in the book of Acts concludes with the church established in Rome, the imperial city, center of the Mediterranean world.

The four Gospels and the book of Acts became two of the main components in the **coming together of the Newer or Second or Christian Testament.** The Gospels and Acts are at the front of the Newer Testament, followed by letters written by Jesus' early followers and a book of visions, called the Apocalypse or Revelation. Chief among the letter writers is Paul, who did the first major reflections on the meaning of Christ Jesus (see the quotation above). The creation of a Newer Testament to go with the Tanakh was a gift basically completed by the start of the second century.

Chapter Two

The Early Church

Struggling Centuries of the Church (110–500 CE)

By the end of the first century CE, those who had known Jesus in person were gone, and the church was already with third- and fourth-generation Christians. These Christians and subsequent followers seemed to be equally fervent for the faith. In time they extended the good news of Christ to the borders of the Roman Empire—and sometimes beyond, as to Ireland and to Persia.

In these early centuries there were periods of struggle and conflict with the Roman authorities. When a Roman emperor, for example, would declare himself to be divine and require subjects to put a pinch of incense on the burning coals before his imperial bust, Christians normally would not do this. So, beginning in the year 64 CE under Emperor Nero and continuing for the next two and a half centuries, there sometimes was **persecution of the church**.

For the most part, persecution was practiced intermittently (in 95, 155, 203, 250, and 303 CE) and regionally (in Asia Minor now, North Africa later, over in Gaul another time, etc.). Even so, many in the early church were arrested, tortured, and killed for their faith, becoming martyrs, that is, "witnesses," to the God made known in Jesus. In spite of hard times, or perhaps because of them, the church grew. Tertullian, an early church figure, said, "The blood of martyrs is seed for the church." So it seemed.

Attempt was also made to give Christianity intellectual and social acceptance. This was part of the struggle too. Christian thinkers, usually bishops, became "apologists" for the faith, explainers. They read the Greek philosophers and looked for areas of compatibility of thought with Christian sources. They proclaimed that Christians were loyal subjects in

13

the empire, though their first loyalty was always to God. They highlighted the moral strengths of faithful Christians. Origen and Clement of Alexandria were two such spokespersons. Some of the apologists ended up as martyrs: Polycarp of Smyrna, Justin of Rome, and Irenaeus of Lyons.

Persecution ended abruptly in the year 313 CE when **AN EDICT OF TOLERATION was given** by Emperors Constantine and Licinius. They let Christianity stand as a legitimate religion. Moreover, Constantine was interested in letting Christianity become a unifying element in the empire. Both Roman state and Christian church were widespread, and he could see that the church was attractive to ordinary folk, his soldiers, and, increasingly, to the intelligentsia. Furthermore, Christians had a social system of care for people, and such a system was greatly needed in the empire. So, toleration—indeed, encouragement— was given the church.

What a rapid turnaround! In Asia Minor near Ephesus there is a Cave of the Seven Sleepers. According to legend, seven boys fled to a mountain cave in 203 CE to escape Roman persecution and fell asleep. They slept for a hundred years. When they awoke, they found that their minority sect was now the majority religion!

The Edict of Toleration, by which persecution ended, is the hinge on which a great new door swung. State and church now began working together. Things proceeded so quickly that by the year 381 Christianity was adopted as the official religion of the empire! This closeness continued through most of the subsequent centuries. Collaboration created what came to be called caesaropapism (the emperor over the patriarch) in the eastern empire and made for western Europe's "Christendom" of the late Middle Ages.

One of the immediate things that toleration did was open the door for church leaders from all over the empire to come together. In 325 CE an **ecumenical council of bishops was held in Nicaea**, near Constantinople, Emperor Constantine's new capital city. Bishops met and decided on church doctrine (belief) and practices. They wrote the Nicene Creed. Further, they agreed on what books would and would not be Christian Scripture. Other councils were held later, at Constantinople in 381, Ephesus in 431, and Chalcedon in 451, starting a long tradition of twenty-one councils over the millennia. Recalling that the Nicene and Chalcedonian creeds are still recited in churches today, one senses the long-term significance of these gatherings.

The councils defined orthodoxy, that is, "right belief," the doctrinal truths to which the faithful should subscribe. The defining was not without disagreement. After Nicaea there were centuries of christological controversy. How, for example, is one to understand Jesus? Is he a man? a godly man? half man/half god? god only but in disguise? born of a virgin? and so on. Orthodox Christians fixed on the paradoxical idea of Christ being "wholly God and wholly Man." As these questions and controversies raged, rifts at first minor, then major, began to show in the church. Nonorthodox believers—gnostics, Manicheans, Arians, Monophysites, and others—were called "heretics" by the orthodox. (See the glossary for some definitions.)

The church fathers and mothers of this period worked hard at defining right beliefs and practices. It is not wrong to say that **acceptance of the work of scholars and theologians** is a development of major long-term Christian consequence. Jerome (connected to Bible translation), Eusebius (the first church historian), and the Cappadocian Fathers and Mother (who wrote on the Trinity) were instrumental in shaping the faith and establishing a reflective tradition. The greatest of the theologians of this period is Augustine, bishop of Hippo in North Africa. He wrote passionately and personally about his faith, including powerful orthodox-defining theological treatises and an interpretation of the meaning of the fall of Rome, which occurred in 410 CE. His understanding of "faith as a free gift of God" will come to rally Christians back to the centrality of grace and faith (over works) many times in the millennia to come.

By the year 500 CE the church was quite strong and, basically, intact. The Mediterranean Sea was a "Christian lake." The faith was predominant in southern Europe, the Middle East, and North Africa; it had spread east into India, west to Ireland, south into Ethiopia and, in foraying ways, was present in central Europe. The blanket of Christianity, though, was being torn and would be radically ripped in the next 500 years.

The Age of Monasticism (500–1100 CE)

There were three **INCURSIONS UPON THE EMPIRE(S)** that did the ripping of the Christian cloth. First and earliest, even before 500, were **the so-called "barbarian" invasions.** Germanic tribes came sweeping into the western Roman Empire from the north and east. Often they obliterated church establishments made in previous centuries, as when the Franks conquered Gaul, the Jutes/Angles/Saxons came to Britain, the Visigoths and Ostrogoths went into Italy and Spain, and the Vandals conquered around to North Africa. (Magyars came late in the millennium, after 800.)

Second, there was **the rise and spread of Islam** from the deserts of Arabia in the seventh century CE. The coming of this major new religion via horses and scimitars had immense and long lasting consequence for Christianity. The population center of the ancient church had been in the Middle East and North Africa, in such cities as Baghdad, Damascus, and Alexandria. Within a hundred years of the time of Islam founder Muhammad's death in 632, these lands went under the control of Arab Muslims. Even European Spain became a Muslim country.

In addition to the Germanic and Arabic incursions, there came a third: **Viking attacks** from the north. Norsemen came out of pagan Scandinavia during the late centuries of the first millennium. They conducted sea raids on Ireland, Britain, and western Europe, entered the Mediterranean, conquering Sicily and southern Italy, and swung around even to rule Black Sea cities (meeting their own who came down the Danube)!

This period of time, especially for western Europe, is often called the Dark Ages. The once-coherent Roman Empire was shattered, and prevailing Christianity was threatened. What we want to note, though, is that in those darkening centuries with incursions from without, there were candle-lighting responses from within that kept faith, learning, and culture alive, that all might come to brighter light in later times.

Faith- and culture-sustaining responses were made by Christians, especially through **monastic life and action**. Monasticism began in the fourth century CE in Egypt and spread throughout the Christian world as a way to keep the faith. Many had felt that authentic Christianity was being compromised when adopted by the worldly, the wealthy, and the powerful. To live more God-centered lives, men fled to the desert to become solitary monks. Other men and women entered into monasteries and convents, living in community and practicing chastity, poverty, and obedience. In the early 500s Benedict of Nursia (in Italy) wrote a rule by which his order and subsequent orders of Western monks and nuns have been governed. Earlier, Basil the Great provided guidance by which monks and nuns of the East were governed even to the present day. The monasteries and convents turned out to be islands of learning and devotion when so much of Christianity and Greco-Roman culture was under assault.

The long-term effective work of Christianity was carried by the monastic orders simply by their very being. Monks and nuns modeled an alternative way of life, which was *ora et labora* ("pray and work"). They drew people to them for physical sanctuary, for intellectual learning, for a model of farming and animal husbandry, for music, art, healing, dying, and much more. The orders demonstrated a "more excellent way" in a terribly rough world.

In due time, the islands of faith became sending stations to replant Christianity. Often the monks were invited to come preach and establish a presence in expanded locations. Just as often they moved on their own, under missionary impulse. The Celtic monks of Ireland, for example, launched a successful campaign west-to-east to reclaim Europe for the faith. Columba landed at Iona, off the coast of Scotland, and moved inland to convert the Picts (Scots). He sent missionaries into northern England and Wales. His associate, Columbanus, went still farther east to establish new monasteries in France and Italy. Over time these monks and their successors went into Germany, Switzerland, North Africa, and even Russia. The Celtic monks elicited help for work in England by getting Pope Gregory the Great to send forty monks under Augustine of Canterbury to Britain. So Christianity came to be practiced by the Anglo-Saxons of Britain.

Across the channel, there was a political turnaround when Clovis, king of the Franks, adopted Christianity as his—and his people's—religion in 496 CE. One of his centuries-later successors, Charles Martel, in 732 CE turned back an invasion by the Arab Muslims. Most significantly, Martel's grandson, Charles the Great (Charlemagne), had by 800 CE formed a **new, extensive Holy Roman Empire**, with the "Holy" part of that title being Christianity. Right alongside Constantine, the turn-around hero 500 years earlier, Charlemagne was put on an enormous equestrian statue inside Saint Peter's Cathedral in Rome for his reunifying success!

In the eastern and southern portions of the empire (as Islamic Arabs swept west), the monasteries continued to function, but they became increasingly isolated and insulated. Islam was *not* destructive of the Christian institutions. In fact, it was remarkably tolerant of both Judaism and Christianity. Over the centuries, though, Christianity was stretched and weakened, and in some places, such as northwest Africa, it disappeared. At first the armies of Islam did not succeed in the Aegean arena, so there continued to be a flowering of Byzantine-Greek Christianity.

As churches of the Middle East and Africa were cut off from the church in Constantinople by the Muslims, the Oecumenical Patriarchs (clergy who headed the Orthodox Church) in Constantinople became mission-minded in new directions. Expansion into central Europe and Russia occurred toward the last of this first millennium CE, the Christian message being carried by traveling monks. Cyril and Methodius, for example, went from Constantinople into Moravia, to what is now the Czech Republic, to kindle the faith. Other monks, on invitation, went to Russia and established the faith with the tsar and his northern people. The **Christianization of Russia** is one of the major developments of Christian history. Today the Russian church makes Orthodoxy the second largest body of Christian believers in the world, exceeded in numbers only by Roman Catholics. In 1988 the Russian people celebrated a thousand years of Christianity.

Thousand-year histories of the faith may be celebrated in northwest Europe too. Missionary monks of the Western church made their way into Scandinavian countries during these centuries, St. Anskar going to Denmark and Sweden in the ninth century.

Though Christian frontiers were expanding, the "one" church of Christ was fracturing. The Catholic church in Rome and the Orthodox church in Constantinople drifted apart. The differences between these two historic "sees" (seats or chairs) were doctrinal, political, cultural, and linguistic. Things got so bad that in the year 1054 CE pope and patriarch exchanged mutual anathemas (curses)! Thus was formalized the **East (Orthodox)-West (Catholic) schism**. The schism had major negative consequence for East-West relations during the later Middle Ages.

As the first millennium CE closed, Western monasticism was strongest in France. From the monastery at Cluny in east central France came continued revitalization of the church's worship life and winning of the hearts of central Europeans back to the faith. This was mostly in the tenth and eleventh centuries. More than a thousand monasteries were birthed from the Cluny motherhouse. When in later years the Cluniacs became complacent, leadership shifted to the Cistercian order of Benedictine monks at Citeaux, France. Cistercians also were missionary-minded and activists in church reform.

High Christendom Years (1100–1450 CE)

By the beginning of the second millennium, the West, generally, and the Western church, in particular, were together and feeling strong again. Though Viking invasions had severely disrupted life, the Norsemen eventually settled down. A primary settling place was northern France, Normandy. These Normans wrested control of Saxon Britain from other Norsemen at the Battle of Hastings in 1066. Whether in Normandy, Britain, Sicily-Italy, or Russia, in due time these ex-Scandinavians also became Christian. By the end of the eleventh century, they were as loyal to the church in Rome as were the powerful Franks. Normans and Franks, then, would respond favorably to a papal invitation to join in a conquest to rescue the Holy Lands when the invitation was issued in 1095. Pope Urban II called for a **holy and armed crusade against the Seljuk Turks,** who were taking over in the east.

The pope's call was answered by hundreds of thousands of western European pilgrims and soldiers. From 1096 to 1291 armies led by kings and knights marched and sailed east and fought with the ostensible goal of capturing and holding sacred sites of the faith. The First Crusade against "the infidels" met with considerable battle success. Jerusalem was taken in 1099. What is not usually told is that the capture of Jerusalem led to the slaughter of 40,000 inhabitants, the majority of whom were *Christians,* albeit Arab Christians. Jerusalem, David's holy city of old, was in the hands of Western knights for about a century.

After the First Crusade, things just got worse for the Franks (as the crusaders were considered). At the Battle of Hattim the Western knights were cut down by Saladin of Egypt. They never fully recovered. Other things went awry too. During the Fourth Crusade of 1204 CE, a Christian Western navy laid siege to Christian Constantinople and, conquering, burned it to the ground! During another Crusade, children gathered at seaports, believing they could liberate Jerusalem in their innocence, but instead were taken off and sold in North Africa as slaves!

Ultimately, of course, all efforts by Western powers to dominate the East proved to be futile. By the start of the fourteenth century, the crusaders were gone, and in 1453 a weakened **Constantinople fell** to Ottoman Turks. Thereafter most of Orthodox, as well as Syrian, Nestorian in Persia, and Coptic in Egypt, Christianity was under Muslim suzerainty. Eventually Greek and Slavic Orthodoxy was overrun. The major exceptions were Ethiopia and Russia. When Constantinople (which had called itself the Second Rome) fell and became Istanbul, Moscow began to call itself the Third Rome.

There is an upside to all this grim history. Western Europeans, by going east and south into Moorish Spain, were exposed to the learning and high culture of both Byzantium and Islam. They began to see new possibilities for themselves, so that **positive transfer of culture to western Europe took place**. The literature, art, and sciences of the ancient Greeks and of Arabic scholars were introduced to the West, ultimately ushering in the Renaissance. Learning took place regarding mathematics, money, government, poetry, architecture, and more. Long-forgotten Greek writings, which Byzantine and Islamic scholars had preserved, managed to be transferred to the West. In particular, the philosophy of Aristotle was presented for Christian consumption and theological reformulation.

For these reasons and others, there was new vitality in the Western church, to wit:

> great Gothic cathedrals arose;
> stained-glass art appeared in churches;
> music became polyphonic;
> cathedral schools became great universities;
> learning and worship flourished in reinvigorated monasteries.

As the pope in Rome and the Holy Roman emperor worked together—and vied for power, at times—**Christendom came to be**. The medieval Roman church of the High Middle Ages became stronger than ever, its great authority suggested by the career of Pope Innocent III, who died 1216 CE. Innocent instituted church reform, deposed and crowned kings, directed armies, established the Inquisition, appointed a westerner to head the Eastern church, and more. To his greatest credit, he approved two new religious orders, the Dominicans and Franciscans. The preaching Dominicans led in scholarship and teaching, while the mendicant Franciscans offered a simpler Christianity, devoted to Mary and serving the poor. They both continue unabated to the present day.

Later, however, there was also severe regression in the church. The corruption of the papacy is sometimes spoken of. At one time, for example, *three* popes reigned. One of the abuses of the church was simony, the sale of church offices (such as a bishopric) to the highest bidder, whether he be cleric or burgher. The church also began to sell indulgences, the purchase of which supposedly rescued lost souls from purgatory. In the early 1400s, John Huss, a Czech educator and priest, protested such abuses and, further, issued a call for return of offering wine to all Christian communicants, not just the priests. Huss was burned at the stake as a heretic. The relevance and truth of what he believed would not be fully received for another century.

Chapter Three

The Later Church

Reformations/New Worlds Era (1450–1650)

On All Souls' Day, 1517 CE, on the cathedral door in the town of Wittenberg, Germany, some students did a **POSTING OF NINETY-FIVE THESES** for debate. The debate propositions, on questions of faith and church practices, were penned by an Augustinian monk and scholar named Martin Luther. One of the theses, No. 36, reads,

> Every Christian who sincerely repents has perfect . . . pardon from
> all punishment and guilt even without an Indulgence.

So began the **Protestant Reformation**. Luther protested *against* abuses of the church and gave testimony *for* a deeper spirituality in which faith, not works, was central. He advocated for new, often renewed, formulation of Christianity, including:

- The authority of the Bible, over popes and councils
- Use of the vernacular, rather than Latin, in worship and preaching
- Preaching as a near-sacrament, alongside Communion
- Communion in *both* kinds (bread *and* wine) for communicants
- The priesthood of all believers, not just persons set aside

Luther was not interested in monasticism as a way of embodying the faith. So convents and monasteries closed—sadly, for women, for this removed one of the few medieval areas allowing for their leadership.

Luther's theses for debate were quickly made known in Europe because of a technological breakthrough, **the invention of the printing**

press, a half-century earlier. By Johannes Gutenberg's appliance, the ideas of Luther and other Protestant Reformers could be made known widely and quickly. The printing press ushered in the print-media age of which we are still heirs—and of which this book is an example.

Joining Luther in reform were John Calvin, Archbishop Thomas Cranmer, and Menno Simons, to name three other persons quite prominent. From their thought and efforts emerged four distinguishable branches of Protestantism (in various countries):

1. Lutheran (Germany, Scandinavia)
2. Reformed (Switzerland, France, Scotland, Holland, Hungary)
3. Anglican (England, Wales)
4. Anabaptist (Switzerland, Moravia, Germany, Holland, usually on the edges)

Over time, in other countries, because of theological, ethnic, class, economic, racial, and other social factors, many subbranches of these four emerged.

Protestantism's break from Rome generated response. Irving Stone's *The Agony and the Ecstasy*, a life of the artist Michelangelo, suggests that Italian popes were more focused on acquiring art than stopping heresy; but that is not quite accurate. A **Catholic Counter-Reformation was launched**. The pope sent a delegate to Germany demanding that Luther recant; a Catholic theologian came to debate him; the pope issued a bull of excommunication; and the Holy Roman emperor, Charles V, had Luther appear before his court. Luther, protected by German princes, stood firm. The church could not rein him in.

Protestantism progressed.

In 1545 the pope called a council to meet in Trent (northern Italy) to deal with issues theological and organizational. By 1563 the council finished its work, making corrections of the church's worst abuses, fixing Catholic doctrine and practices, and organizing effort to reverse Protestant inroads. The reversal effort was headed by a new religious order, the Society of Jesus, otherwise known as the Jesuits. Jesuits effectively countered Protestant advances in Spain, Italy, and Austria, and they led in reform of the Catholic Church generally.

Verbal and written conflict soon turned physical. In the seventeenth century the bloody Thirty Years' War was fought by the several "Christian" parties in central Europe. It was finally brought to end by the Peace of Westphalia in 1648, through an idea put forward a century earlier in the concept of *cuius regio, eius religio*, that is, "whoever rules a region shall determine its religion." Princes in northern Germany, for example, generally opted for Lutheranism, while those in Bavaria went Catholic. Some regions went to Reformed princes, as in Holland, Switzerland, and Hungary. Anabaptists had few places to land, but persevered though persecuted. By the year 1648, all sides were exhausted by the bloodshed. For many people, doubt certainly arose as to whether religious dogma was worth killing for. In Poland, finally—and elsewhere, slowly—came the idea of tolerating persons of differing religious persuasion.

Beyond war and in addition to princely decision and late-arriving policies of tolerance, another way of handling religious pluralism was found. Some people in Europe began to direct their religious enthusiasm by starting over in a new place. Consideration of moving was possible because of one central event: **DISCOVERY OF THE NEW WORLD**. In 1492 Christopher Columbus for Spain confirmed that there was "a whole other (round) world out there"! In 1498 Vasco da Gama of Portugal rounded the Cape of Good Hope in Africa and opened the European Occident to the Orient. Such naval feats opened doors for change in the Christianity to come. The discoverers expanded European and Christian horizons. To settle Spanish-Portuguese territorial disputes, the pope drew a line down the Atlantic and told the Portuguese to work in Brazil and *east* and the Spaniards to go *west*.

Going into the Americas with the conquistadors were the Dominicans and Franciscans, who traveled into the West Indies, Mexico, South America, and even California. Jesuits went with French explorers into Canada. The fathers and friars who accompanied explorers, conquerors, gold-seekers, traders, fur trappers, and so forth went along as chaplains to the main players *and* to win native peoples to the faith. Their means were sometimes the sword or offer of food but also—for which we are thankful—love of and service to those with whom they worked. As indication of the sincerity of their work, most missionaries asked to be buried in the soil of the land of the people with whom they worked.

Jesuit fathers began to work their way into Brazil, but their missionary effort was not restricted to the western hemisphere. Francis Xavier (perhaps the best known missionary since Paul) took the faith to India, Sri Lanka, and Japan. Father Matteo Ricci served successfully in China.

If Catholic religious orders primarily went out to proselytize, Protestant groups went into the New World to settle and make a new life for themselves and their children. Conversion of original inhabitants was a secondary concern. North America, in particular, offered Protestants an "escape place" for setup of their New Jerusalems. Along the Atlantic seaboard, early emigrant people could build faith communities almost as they willed, somewhat isolated, and not in conflict with others. The early American colonies had relatively clear denominational lines. Anglicans were in the south, Presbyterians and Quakers in the middle colonies, Dutch Reformed people in New York, and Congregationalists in New England. There were a few Catholics and Jews in Maryland. When religious disputes arose, differences were not usually resolved by armed conflict, as in Europe, but by one group moving "into the wilderness." Only in America could this happen. If families went west without institution and benefit of clergy, their frontier settlements were served by "saddlebag preachers." Such preachers became main players for Methodists and Baptists in the eighteenth and nineteenth centuries.

Westward movement of white Europeans, of course, usually meant that Native Americans suffered. Indian people generally took to Christianity quite slowly. Not so with **black African slaves introduced to America**. Taken to the West Indies and Virginia even before the Pilgrims landed, they adopted Christianity—or adapted it to West African religion—rather quickly. "Church" was one institution of some freedom and self-expression for them in the culture of slavery. They shared the Bible account of Moses and exodus in song, aspiration, and action till freedom finally was gained centuries later.

During the nineteenth century, Protestants in America, Britain, and northern Europe began to follow their Catholic counterparts and use the sea lanes of the world to take their versions of the faith everywhere. Historian Kenneth Scott Latourette describes the 1800s as "the greatest century which Christianity had thus far known."[1] Much of this must be attributed to **renewed commitment to mission** with new awareness of worlds and peoples beyond. All continents and the people therein were recipients of missionaries who accompanied colonial powers, or were sent by national or denominational missionary societies . . . or went on their own. The most famous of the nineteenth-century missionaries was David Livingstone, who went to what is now Botswana in Africa on behalf of the London Missionary Society. There he won the confidence of the people by his medical work and schools. Later he did exploration into the African interior and was, for a time, thought lost. He was found, though, by H. M. Stanley of the *New York Herald*, who greeted him with the famous words, "Dr. Livingstone, I presume?!"

In discussing the nineteenth century, we are ahead of our story, but the effect of discovering new worlds and the reaching out to its many people can be concluded here, though ahead of our chronology. By the time the third millennium was reached, Christianity had wrapped the globe well and was hugely successful in terms of gaining disciples. Approximately 2 billion adherents to Jesus Christ are in the world today, constituting about a third of the earth's population. Most fascinating of all is the fact that Christians in Europe and North America are now outnumbered by Christians in the rest of the world. There are 301 million Christians in Asia and its southern rim, compared with 220 million who live in North America!

The Ecumenical Age (1650 CE–Present)

Our faith has had frontiers other than geographic with which to deal.

AN APPLE FELL from a tree in 1665, and according to legend the person who observed the fall, Isaac Newton, grasped "the law of universal gravitation." With Newton's unified field theory in mechanics, his seminal work in mathematics (inventing calculus), astronomy, optics, and other fields, we can talk about **THE RISE OF SCIENCE**. Science, more than anything else, has created the modern world and been the foil for much of faith's fencing in recent centuries.

By 1650 the religious wars had ended in Europe, and the work of Copernicus, Galileo, Bacon, and others was making an impact, leading to the "falling apple" symbol for science and Sir Isaac Newton. The greatest minds of the time now thought less about "the world beyond" and much more about "this physical universe." At best, they, like Newton, said they were "thinking God's thoughts after him," but the Christian God was not necessary to explain the world. Moreover, much about the Bible, theological doctrines, and religious institutions needed rethinking, if not outright changing. More and more, "man" became the measure of all things. People's faith was placed in *homo solo* (human ability alone) to shape and fix the world. Inductive and investigative sciences were the rage.

One early and ongoing reaction to scientific theory and findings for some Christians was just that: reaction. Some clerics saw science as a threat to faith. A Catholic council denounced Galileo for being too willing to say it was a "fact" that planets revolve around the sun. (The Catholic Church did not rescind its judgment on the subject and Galileo till late in the twentieth century.) Considerable ideological controversy also ensued about the thought and findings of four people whom church historian Martin Marty dubs as "the bearded God-killers": Charles Darwin (evolution), Karl Marx (class and economics),

Friedrich Nietzsche (philosophy), and Sigmund Freud (psychology). These four intellectual giants made contributions to the world that have been most influential.

Some quarters of the church went into strong denial over scientific theory and findings, as signaled in the famous "Monkey Trial" of 1925 in Tennessee and by contemporary efforts of some Christians to introduce "creationism" into the schools.

Other Christians, however, were open to scientific work, welcoming it, advancing it. In the twentieth century Teilhard de Chardin, a Jesuit priest and paleontologist, said that evolutionary anthropology is the way God is working in time. Process theology, which sprang from the thought of mathematician Alfred North Whitehead, has enabled Christian thinkers to work within the scientific worldview. Interestingly enough, in the last century physicists turned science away from an earlier, Newtonian mechanistic understanding of the universe and began to rely on quantum physics with talk of uncertainty, relativity, and change. Some physicists even suggest that "love" is the foundational element of the universe. What an opening this has been to Christian theologians who might now talk about God's ongoing creativity through love!

Accompanying science and technology to make up modernity has been **the Age of Reason**, also known as **the Enlightenment**. Enlightenment reasoning was "the way to think" during the eighteenth century in France, Germany, and England. It spilled west into America. Reason, nature, and natural law were thought sufficient for humans. There was no need for religious superstition or supposed revelation. Sophisticated folk became "cultured despisers" of religion; that was what Friedrich Schleiermacher saw happening in Germany. Zealous "rationalists" in France became church burners. Some Enlightenment folk became agnostics, if not atheists; others went into deism or unitarianism for a religious stance.

The primary response of Christians to the rise of science and of the Enlightenment was and has been that **the faithful gave themselves to a "religion of the heart."** Blaise Pascal said it best: "The heart has reasons that reason knows not of." Heartfelt religion, or Pietism, sprang up in Germany and influenced all the denominations. Methodism, which arose in eighteenth-century England, certainly had "heartwarming" at its center. In Catholic circles a new appreciation of "the numinous" came back with the mystics of Spain and popular devotion to Mary. In Protestant theological understanding, religion came to be defined as "the feeling of absolute dependence on God" (Schleiermacher), and the whole feeling/

emotional/psychological understanding of the faith is how things went. It is where things are yet in the church.

The above, especially the impact of the Enlightenment, can be presented in another way, that is, with regard to politics and society. In the coming-together United States, the most influential leaders (Madison and Jefferson, for example) were men of the Enlightenment. Madison helped birth the Constitution in 1787. One of the important events that gave new shape to religion in this country was **creation of the doctrine of the separation of church and state**. This separation was written into the Constitution's Bill of Rights: "Congress shall make no law respecting an establishment of religion, or prohibiting the free exercise thereof." That signaled a major change, as nine of the original thirteen colonies had "established" religions. With this separation idea, official support of churches in individual states soon ended, obliging the faithful to discover new ways of maintaining churches and being faithful. No longer supported by the taxes of government, religious institutions had to "take their case to the people." **Evangelical revivalism** came to be an American institution in ways that had not existed in other countries so strongly. In addition, the following can be listed as distinctive characteristics of American Christianity:

- Reliance on volunteerism
- Highlighting social life (fellowship, community)
- The lay-led Sunday school movement
- Age-focused ministries, e.g., to youth
- Emphasis on the stewardship of money
- Stress on the individual, psychological preaching
- Continuous attempts to be new and relevant

The condition of being "cut free" from the state and having to "sink or swim" made American Christian churches more vital (though perhaps shallower) than those of European coreligionists. Statistically, Christianity in the United States was successful. At the start of the 1800s, it is estimated that only 5 percent of the citizenry was church-affiliated; by 1950 the percentage was 65 percent. It has stayed near that level for the last fifty years. Father Andrew Greeley in his book *Religion in the Year 2000* (written 30 years ago) said churches would be around in strength by this year (now plus!). He seems to have been correct.

Freedom of and for religion in America brought about **the proliferation of denominations**. The process began early in United States history, so that before 1850 the Adventists, Disciples, Mormons, and Unitarians—shorthand names for all—came on the scene. The process continued to the present, new religious groups created yearly. The 2003 *Yearbook of American and Canadian Churches* shows eighteen denominations in the family of Eastern Orthodox Churches, twenty-one varieties of Baptists, and thirty-one Pentecostal bodies. In America there are more than three thousand identified denominations, in the world almost 40,000! Beyond or outside denominational families, there are "free" or stand-alone institutions that call themselves nondenominational churches. Some are megachurches, so big in size they can function like a denomination.

Whether churches belong to denominations or are stand-alones, there are developments and movements that overlay them and give shape to the religious picture. Consider (without definition here) the following:

the social gospel
fundamentalism
the liturgical renewal
resurgence of spirituality
liberation theologies
parachurch organizations

There are others, including the **charismatic-pentecostal movement**, which has enjoyed a worldwide explosion in the last century, and **Christian feminism**, which is having immense impact on the shape of the church now and for the foreseeable future.

Ahead of all the above-listed developments, I want to believe, is **the ecumenical movement**, the drawing together of Christ's divided house. Twentieth-century Archbishop of Canterbury William Temple calls the coming together of churches "the great new fact of our era." It began early in the last century by fractured Protestants moving toward one another, and it came to early fulfillment on the mission fields, where denominationalism was failing and cooperation was found to be a better way. So in 1948 the Church of South India, for example, came to be. The event that symbolizes this great new fact for many is **VATICAN II**, the Roman Catholic ecumenical council that met in the 1960s. Pope John XXIII called Catholic bishops from around the world to consider renewal of church thought and practice. Among important aspects to this council was expressed openness to other Christians of the world. Ecumenism began to work: in 1979 Pope John Paul II of Rome and the Orthodox oecu-

The Later Church   29

menical patriarch, Dimitrios I, of Constantinople attended each other's liturgies and, essentially, negated the mutual anathemas given in 1054! Pontiff and patriarch physically embraced. An ongoing ecumenical commission of Orthodox and Catholic Christians began.

What happened for Catholics went on for other branches of the church today and for some time, as in the Faith and Order meetings of the World Council of Churches and its precursors. We can observe churches widely separated for hundreds of years coming back together. Lutherans and Episcopalians, to give just one current example, say they are of one mind now on church government and Communion. In a recent pamphlet issued by the Waldensian Church, greatly persecuted in the twelfth century, these words are found:

> [R]elations with the Roman Catholic Church were controversial until the Second Vatican Council (1962–1965), when the idea developed in Italy of a more open attitude toward religion between the churches.

Commitment to the ecumenical movement feels not as strong as it was a decade or two ago. Nevertheless, it continues, often at local levels as pastors and laypeople come together at table for study and meal sharing. There are conversation, cooperation, and some confluence, as suggested in the following church relations:

- Intradenominational (reunions within church families, e.g., nationality-divided Lutherans, or north-south region Presbyterians and Methodists)
- Interdenominational (Disciples–United Church of Christ merger talks, Churches Uniting in Christ [formerly the Consultation on Church Union], and more conservative Christians in the National Association of Evangelicals)
- Orthodox-Catholic-Protestant (Orthodox involvement in the World Council of Churches, Catholic participation in local councils of churches, and Protestant observers at Vatican conferences)

And there is dialogue by Christians with Jews, Muslims, and leaders of other world religions, especially since September 11, 2001. Truly now the "whole civilized world" (*oecumene*) is engaging in finding common roots and appreciating the different realities that sustain each.

Conclusion to Part 1

On the third Sunday in October each year, First Congregational United Church of Christ in Colorado Springs (the church I have served) observes Historical Sunday. Pastors and people celebrate the start of the church in 1874, and members remember the important events that have sustained and set back the church over the years. Sometimes, when we gather round the table to break bread, there is a sense that our short history stands within a much larger continuum, dating back to celebrations around a campfire in the hill country of central Palestine 1200 BCE. When we are at our best, we appreciate being nourished by a temple in Jerusalem, a sacred text born of difficulty, a savior nonpareil, an emperor's conversion, monks and nuns at prayer and work, theses for debate, seafaring pilgrims, "a heart strangely warmed" . . . and **GOD MAKING ALL THINGS NEW**.

Discussion Questions for Part 1: Central Historical Events

1. Do you agree with the author on the ten most important events (p. 2) of our faith's history? How would you rank them (one to ten)? What would you add or delete?

2. Daring to share personal histories, can you recall "a big door that swung on a little hinge" for you? Have all life-changing events been positive? Have some been disastrous, or seemingly so at the time?

3. In the life of your local church, what do you know have been decisive moments? Can you think, not only of individuals, but of events or forces that caused change (an endowment, flood, changing neighborhood, relocation, etc.)?

4. A historian once described the calamitous fourteenth century in Europe as a "distant mirror." Do you see events and things from the history of the Christian church that seem to mirror present-day developments. What are they?

Time Line

Before the Common Era (BCE)

Premonarchic Millennium

(Many dates of this period are "various")

←October, 4004 Creation (according to Archbishop Ussher, seventeenth
                century)
←3941   Adam and Eve (one Bible chronology)
←2348   The flood and Noah
←2100   Ziggurat built in Ur
1995/85   Abram/Sarai born in Mesopotamia
                Migration to Canaan
±1800   Isaac and Rebekah, Jacob and wives and sons
1728   Hammurabi of Babylon's law code
±1700   Joseph, then Israel, in Egypt
1379   Pharaoh Akhenaton reigns in Egypt
                Rule of EGYPTIANS
1275   **Moses, EXODUS EVENT**
                Sinai wilderness, Ten Commandments
1200   Joshua and battle of Jericho
                "Conquest" of Canaan
1100   Judges Gideon, Deborah, Samson

Time of the Kings and the Prophets

1025   Samuel anoints Saul king, later David
1000   **David, ESTABLISHING JERUSALEM**
954   **Solomon, BUILDING TEMPLE**
926   Kingdom splits into north and south

31

860	Prophets Elijah and Elisha active
700s	Writing prophets: Amos, Hosea, Micah
753	Founding of Rome
742	First Isaiah begins career
722	**Northern kingdom (Samaria) falls**
	Rule of ASSYRIANS
600s	Camels become important transportation
628	Jeremiah the prophet begins long career
621	King Josiah's reforms (Deuteronomy)
612	Babylonians defeat Assyrians at Nineveh
586	**Destruction of Jerusalem and Temple**
	EXILE in Babylon, Diaspora
	Rule of BABYLONIANS
550	Second Isaiah's oracles of hope

Second Temple Period

538	**Cyrus the Persian ends exile**
	Jews in Babylon RETURN home
	Rule of PERSIANS
516	Zerubbabel completes temple in Jerusalem
490	Greeks defeat Persians at Marathon
445	Wall built around Jerusalem; Nehemiah
±440	The Law enforced by Ezra
5th/4th cent.	**Bible's Law and Prophets finalized**
5th/4th cent.	In Greece: Socrates, Plato, Aristotle
333	Alexander the Great conquers Persia
332	Jerusalem taken, Alexandria founded
	Rule of GREEKS, Ptolemies, then Seleucids
250	Bible translated into Greek (Septuagint)
167–142	Maccabean revolt in Judah
	Rule by HASMONEAN kings
125	With **Writings**, Older Testament complete
63	Pompey takes Jerusalem
	Rule of ROMANS
40	Herod the Idumean made king
20	Temple "of Herod" completed
06 or 04	Jesus of Nazareth born in Bethlehem

Common Era (CE)

Newer Testament Times

30	**RESURRECTION OF JESUS**
	Foundation of the church at Pentecost
35	Conversion of Saul to Paul = missionary journeys
49	Council of Jerusalem on Gentile inclusion
50	Earliest epistles of Paul
64	Nero persecutes Christians
	Death of Peter and Paul in Rome
±70	First Gospel, Mark, written
	Matthew, Luke, and John follow
70	Titus destroys Jerusalem after rebellion
90	Rabbis at Jamnia = Older Testament canon
	Christians excluded from synagogues
±95	John on Patmos writes Revelation
100	*Didache* (Teaching) written
135	Romans put down Bar Kokhba rebellion = Jews excluded from Jerusalem and Judea

Struggling Centuries of the Church

150	Hippolytus, *Apostolic Tradition*
150	Apostles' Creed first appears
155	Polycarp martyred
200s	Apologists writing: Irenaeus, Justin, Tertullian, Clement, others
250	Emperor Decius's empirewide persecution
270	Antony goes to desert of Egypt
303	Emperor Diocletian's "Great Persecution"
313	**EDICT OF MILAN = TOLERATION for Christians**
320	Pachomius = Communal Monasticism
325	First Ecumenical Council, Nicaea: Nicene Creed declares for Trinity
330	Constantinople becomes imperial capital
358	Basil the Great founds monastery in East
367	Athanasius defines Newer Testament canon
±375	Cappadocians doing orthodox theology

381	Second Ecumenical Council, Constantinople; Christianity becomes state religion
400s	Germanic tribes invading empire
405	Jerome completes Vulgate (Latin) Bible
410	Fall of Rome to Visigoths
	Augustine of Hippo, *City of God*
426	Romans leave Britain to pagan Saxons
432	Patrick to Ireland
450	**GERMANIC INCURSIONS** increase
451	Fourth Ecumenical Council, Chalcedon: Christ declared fully man/fully God
452	Pope Leo I saves Rome from Attila the Hun
476	Last "Roman" emperor
	East ruled by BYZANTINE emperors
	Traditional start of Dark Ages
496	Clovis the Frank baptized

The Age of Monasticism

500s	Dionysius the Pseudo-Areopagite writes
527	Justinian and Theodora rule Byzantium
537	Hagia Sophia built in Constantinople
540	**Benedict's Rule for monks; Monasticism the primary Christian form**
550	First bells in churches, France
564	Columba and Celtic monks begin mission east
589	Synod of Toledo: *filioque* clause in creed
590	Pope Gregory the Great = Gregorian chants
596	Augustine (of Canterbury) arrives England
630	Nestorian Christians in China
622	Muhammad of Arabia = Rise of ISLAM from Arabia
	ISLAMIC INCURSIONS
637	Jerusalem captured, 640 Alexandria library burned, North Africa and Spain taken
664	Synod of Whitby: Roman practices prevail over Celtic practices; date for Easter set
716	Boniface's mission to the Germans
726	Emperor Leo and start of iconoclastic controversies
730	First known church organ

732	Charles Martel stops Muslims at Tours
787	Last of the seven ecumenical councils
800s	**VIKING INCURSIONS** on western Europe
800	Charlemagne crowned emperor
	HOLY ROMAN EMPIRE of West
	Rule by the FRANKS
832	Anskar "Apostle to the North" in Denmark
843	Decree ending iconoclastic controversies
862	Cyril and Methodius's mission to Bohemia
870	Prince Boris of Bulgars adopts Christianity
896	Magyar invasions from Hungary begin
905	Vikings take Normandy, later southern Italy
909	Monastery at Cluny founded
950	King Harold Bluetooth of Denmark baptized
955	Otto the Great defeats Magyars
966	Prince Mieczyslaw of Poland baptized
988	Christianity in Russia at Kiev
1000	Slavs, Bulgars, others are Christian
	Relatively CHRISTIAN EUROPE
1054	Churches East and West split
1066	Battle of Hastings = Norman England

High Christendom Years

1095	Pope Urban II calls for Holy Crusade;
	start of two centuries of war in Holy Land
1098	Anselm, *Cur Deus Homo*
1111	Bernard and Cistercian order of monks
1122	Investiture controversy settled at Worms
1141	Hildegard of Bingen writing and singing
1150	University of Paris founded; Oxford 1190
1187	Saladin retakes Jerusalem from crusaders
1204	Crusaders sack Constantinople
1215	Magna Carta signed = English liberty
1216	Dominic = Dominicans
1223	Francis of Assisi = Franciscans
1260	Chartres cathedral built
1272	Thomas Aquinas, *Summa Theologiae*

1291	Crusaders leave Acre, Crusades end
1300s	Black Death plagues in Europe
1302	Bull *Unam Sanctum* = Pope's supremacy
1309	Avignon, France, "captivity of papacy"
1321	Dante, *Divine Comedy*
14th cent.	Unknown monk, *Cloud of Unknowing*
1375	Wycliffe translates Bible into English
1378	Great papal schism (till 1414)
1400s	RENAISSANCE begins in Italy
1415	John Huss burned at stake
1418	Thomas à Kempis, *Imitation of Christ*
1431	Joan of Arc burned at the stake

Reformations/New Worlds Era

1453	Constantinople falls to Ottoman Turks
1456	Gutenberg = printing press = *Psalter*
1492	**Columbus DISCOVERY OF THE NEW WORLD**
1498	Vasco da Gama rounds Cape of Good Hope MARITIME culture begins
1512	Michelangelo completes Sistine Chapel
1514	Bartolomé de Las Casas argues for Native Americans
1517	**Martin Luther POSTING NINETY-FIVE THESES FOR DEBATE** PROTESTANT REFORMATION begins
1519	Aztecs conquered by Cortés
1525	Anabaptist movement has its start
1531	Juan Diego version of Our Lady of Guadalupe
1533	Henry VIII of England breaks with Rome = Church of England
1536	John Calvin, *Institutes of the Christian Religion* Reformed branch of Protestantism
1543	**Copernican revolution = Solar universe**
1540	Ignatius of Loyola = Jesuits and missions
1545–63	Council of Trent = Catholic Counter-Reformation
1549	*Book of Common Prayer*, first edition
1559	John Knox to Scotland = Presbyterianism
1572	St. Bartholomew's Day Massacre, part of France's suppression of the Huguenots

1589	**Moscow patriarch, "Third Rome," arises**
1603	Virginia plantation colony, Jamestown
1609	John Smythe baptizes self/others = Baptists
1611	King James Version of Bible printed
1620	Pilgrims land on Plymouth Rock, America
1633	Galileo condemned (and Copernican thought)
1639	Roger Williams and First Baptist Church, RI
1647	George Fox = Society of Friends (Quakers)
1648	Peace of Westphalia ends Thirty Years' War

The Ecumenical Age

1658	Cromwell's Puritan rule in England
1664	Restoration of monarchy in England
1665	Isaac Newton = theory of gravitation
	AN APPLE FALLS = RISE OF SCIENCE
1693	(September 11!) Turks defeated at Vienna
1700s	AGE OF REASON/ENLIGHTENMENT
1727	J. S. Bach, *St. Matthew Passion*
1738	John and Charles Wesley = Methodism
1740s	The Great Awakening in America
1765	Steam engine invented
	INDUSTRIAL REVOLUTION under way
1780	Robert Raikes's Sunday school, England
1789	U.S. Constitution and Bill of Rights = **Separation of church and state in America**
1800s	Protestant missionaries to all the world
1801	Cane Ridge = Second Great Awakening
1821	Schleiermacher, *Christian Faith*
1832	Christian Church (Disciples of Christ)
1848	Karl Marx, *Communist Manifesto*
1851	Harriet B. Stowe, *Uncle Tom's Cabin*
1854	Immaculate conception of Mary declared
1859	Darwin, *On the Origin of the Species*
1870	Vatican Council I: Papal infallibility
1890s	Start of social gospel movement
1906	Azusa Street (Pentecostal) revival
1910	Edinburgh Conference on missions

1910	*The Fundamentals* = Fundamentalism
1917	Russian Communist revolution
1919	Karl Barth, *Commentary on Romans* = Neo-orthodoxy
1934	German Confessing Church rejects Nazism
1948	World Council of Churches organized
1962–65	**VATICAN COUNCIL II, ROME**
1963	M. L. King Jr.'s March on Washington
1968	Catholic Bishops' Conference, Medellín, Colombia = Liberation Theology
1970	First Earth Day
1989	Communist regimes ending in Europe
1990s	Christian feminism growing

Part 2

God

O LORD, our Sovereign,
  how majestic is your name in all the earth!
You have set your glory above the heavens.
                                    Psalm 8:1

The human idea of God has a history, since it has always meant
something slightly different to each group of people who have used
it at various points of time. The idea of God formed in one generation by one set of human beings could be meaningless in another.
Indeed, the statement "I believe in God" has no objective meaning, as such, but like any other statement only means something in
context, when proclaimed by a particular community.
                            Karen Armstrong, *A History of God*[1]

Discussion about God should begin with the words of Blaise Pascal,
Christian theologian of the seventeenth century: "The religion that does
not, first of all, assert the mystery of God is a lie." Not wanting to lie, let
me say up front that, in this part, we are dealing with the Ineffable Other,
the One Who Is Beyond Words, the Mystery. That is Whom we want to
talk about, knowing all the while the truth that religious-art historian
Heinrich Zimmer shared:

The best thing cannot be talked about.
The second best thing always will be misunderstood.
And the third isn't worth discussing.

Said humorously in a proverb: "He who hammers above his head will
always hit the nail . . . right on the thumb"!

Still, we shall hammer.

Theology—literally, "talk about God"—is an attempt to put our experience of the Holy into words and concepts. It has been so through the centuries. How we today experience and think about God is rooted in the experiences and thinking of our parents in the faith. We hope that our understanding, worship, and life with God will be aided by recalling our history with God.

As God is mystery, we can not "get at" God directly. Feminist theologian Elizabeth Johnson says, "[T] he experience of God which is never directly available is mediated . . . through the changing history of oneself."[2] It is my contention in these pages that *God is always mediated*. I believe that some thing, some phenomenon, some idea, some something (a physical thing under the sun . . . to a dream thing deep in the night) always stands between us and God. There are mystics, to be sure, who contend we can know God in and of God's self, but I am of a mind with Pope Gregory the Great that there is no way we can talk about God familiarly, as though we had something in common. We are in darkness, yet God illumines us through various physical, conceptual, artistic, and emotional phenomena. Whatever is in between can help both our understanding of and response to God.

In the following three chapters, as in other parts of the book, we are telling the whole four thousand years of biblical and ecclesial (church) history, and here the theme we run with is that of "GOD." I believe the reader will discover that God has been mediated in many ways over the millennia, that the ways may change in different circumstances and times. Some things do not make much sense or appeal to us now, but they did make a great deal of sense in those previous times and circumstances. Having said this, I also want to say that much of that past reflection and experience of God *is* relevant to us, even though we are separated from it by hundreds of years.

Let us proceed, then, with a theological trajectory through the nine periods of faith history we have followed in part 1 of this book. As we go, please note that the GENERAL CATEGORIES to which mediating phenomena belong are in caps, and words for specific "**things**" that seem to be holy-related, important, and communicative of the Mystery are in bold type. To wit: NATURAL PHENOMENON/**thunderclap** as on the facing page.

Chapter Four

God in Biblical Times

Premonarchic Millennium (2000–1000 BCE)

(During this time polytheism, henotheism, and monotheism may be seen, and the names of God, such as *El* and *Yahweh*, emerge.)

In primitive cultures, some kind of animism or polytheism, totem worship with plural gods of nature, precedes the development of more singular views of God. Awe is where it all could begin. A **thunderclap** (powerful NATURAL PHENOMENON) from the sky may have prompted our earliest ancestors to think, "I am not alone in the universe. There are powers, awesome powers, beyond me." During the earliest period of Israel's history (1800 to 1100 BCE), the nomadic Israelites had "their" God of the mountain, perhaps related even to thunder. An early name for that God was **El Shaddai**, meaning "One of the Mountain" (and twenty-first-century people still find God in "mountaintop" experiences). *El* meaning "God" is the first name that our faithparents used of the Holy. The noun *El* takes several adjectives:

> **El Elyon** ("God Most High")
> **El Olam** ("God Everlasting")
> **El Elohe Israel** ("El the God of Israel").

Over the centuries much will be made over the NAME OF GOD, a general category that affects the human-divine relationship.

REVELATORY MOMENTS also give insight into God. One example of a revelatory moment is when progenitor-of-the-faith Moses herding his father-in-law's sheep on the mountain, discovers a **burning bush** which,

41

though burning, is not consumed. In essence the fiery bush is an epiphany, a manifestation of God to him. In Moses' encounter with God he learns two things: (1) his mission to lead the people of Israel out of Egypt and (2) a new name for God, **Yahweh**, translated in the Bible as "LORD."

> Moses said to God, "If I come to the Israelites and say to them, 'The God of your ancestors has sent me to you,' and they ask me, 'What is his name?' what shall I say to them?" God said to Moses, "I AM WHO I AM" [or, I AM WHAT I AM or I WILL BE WHAT I WILL BE or YAHWEH]. (Exod. 3:13–14)

The name for God is very important for Moses, for the people of Israel, and for others through the centuries—right to the present. By invoking the name, the Holy One behind the name is brought near with power to affect the believer's life.

Clarity about who the God of Isra-*El* is comes through in the **exodus EVENT**, an escape from Egypt by an enslaved people. They interpreted escape from bondage as a powerful act of God. God's gracious action made them into a people, and becoming a people was for them the greatest miracle they could imagine. "With a mighty hand and an outstretched arm," they affirmed, "Yahweh led us out of bondage that we might serve him." Theologically, this deliverance meant to them that God was **one who acted** on behalf of the oppressed.

Over time, Moses' name for the LORD, *Yahweh*, is tied in with the older *El* names, names associated with their legendary patriarchs and matriarchs, Abraham and Sarah, Isaac and Rebekah, Jacob and Rachel. *Yahweh*, though, comes to be the most sacred name, always used with care. At Mount Sinai, when Moses receives the Ten Commandments, the third commandment is, "You shall not take the name of the LORD your God in vain" (that is, lightly or sacrilegiously).

Besides names, there also are OBJECTS—physical things—that are invested with holy importance. We think today of amulets worn by bush-people or "Mum's sainted rosary." Few believers would say such things are God, but one might say, "Through this holy object, I access the Holy," or, conversely, "the Holy One accesses me." **The Ten Commandments on stone tablets** and **the ark of the covenant** (for carrying the tablets) are two holy objects that connected the Israelites with God. The Israelites affirmed that God was the one who gave the tablets to Moses. The ark was also invested with an aura of holiness, so much so that anyone who touched it was supposed to be struck dead. Thus it was carried on long poles.

The Ten Commandments had been given on **Mount Sinai,** which was considered a HOLY PLACE. Two other such places should be mentioned for this period. One is **the tabernacle,** which is the ground (albeit movable) wherever the ark-with-tablets was placed; it prefigures a still-to-come temple site. Most important of all places, though, is **the promised land,** the land of Palestine on the eastern Mediterranean, the land into which the people of Israel were led after forty years of wandering in the wilderness. They affirmed it as "a land flowing with milk and honey." PLACE becomes very early, then, a category for mediating God. It will continue to be so throughout subsequent faith history.

For this earliest period, the kind of theology practiced is what in academic circles is called "henotheism," a belief that there are multiple gods but one who is the most powerful. One of the ways henotheism worked is seen in terms of the Bible's battle imagery. Whenever there was an earthly battle, as with another tribe, God (El, Yahweh) was present fighting in the heavens against the enemy god. Such is the imagery of the book of Joshua when Moses' successor, Joshua, took the city of Jericho, and of the book of Judges, when various tribal leaders, male and female, fought for Yahweh and for Israel. Henotheism means, "Our God is greater than other gods."

We may have in this second millennium BCE, though, an incipient monotheism, belief in one God. Sigmund Freud, in his book *Moses and Monotheism,* suggests that Moses was influenced to think of one God because of exposure to the Egyptian Pharaoh Akhenaton's sun god, Re. Re was a singular deity worshipped in Egypt in the mid-1300s BCE, close to the time that Moses was in action. For me, looking to the Kenites of the Sinai Desert for introduction to monotheism makes somewhat more sense. Moses' father-in-law, Jethro the Kenite, lived beneath a big sky near the vastness of a semibarren desert. He could easily be drawn to belief in oneness for the Godhead from that more unitary EXPERIENCE. In any case, Yahweh begins to appear monotheistically around the time that Moses comes under Jethro's influence.

Time of the Kings and the Prophets (1000–550 BCE)

(During this time God is especially mediated by persons and places; ethics are clearly connected to God in radical monotheism; and tragic events occasion God-thought.)

According to the Older Testament story, toward the year 1000 BCE, a cry arose among the beleaguered people of Israel for a **king** to lead them. The prophet Samuel anointed "Tall" Saul to fill that position and then, later,

"Little" David of the house of Jesse (hometown, Bethlehem). That Samuel, a prophet of Yahweh, did the anointing in the name of God suggests that the anointed person was invested with sanctity, filled a DIVINE ROLE. The king and the king's welfare became valued. He was a representative of God on earth, a significant mediator of Yahweh. It is not, therefore, insignificant that monarchs were called "sovereign," and they were so regarded, at least until the eighteenth century CE, when divine heads began to roll. For the people of Israel, David was considered Yahweh's man on earth and would remain the ideal king in their imagination. On behalf of the people Israel, David entered into a **covenant** with Yahweh, which covenant was thought to be forever protective of David's royal city and his people.

The **city of Jerusalem** in the promised land is a PLACE most sacred. Though literally named "City of Peace," Jerusalem has regularly been a city of war, captured in battle some thirty-five times in its four-thousand-plus-year history. At the time of David, Jerusalem belonged to no tribe of Israel but to a people called the Jebusites. David took it from them in the year 1004 BCE and made Jerusalem the capital for the twelve tribes of Israel. Insofar as they all owned it, the tribes were united as one people. The city, also called Zion, came to be considered the abiding place of God, holy—if not virtually identical with God:

> Walk about Zion, go all around it,
>   count its towers,
> consider well its ramparts;
>   go through its citadels,
> that you may tell the next generation
>   that **this is God**,
> our God forever and ever.
>   Ps. 48:12–14

Karen Armstrong in *A History of God* notes that, earlier on, Babylon in Mesopotamia was also considered holy. City-as-sanctified will continue in places like Rome, Constantinople, Moscow, Geneva, even Salt Lake City. Often enough, holy cities are considered "thin places," locations where the wall separating the divine from humans is porous. The point is that a city, in this case Jerusalem, is a sacred place, mediating God.

The writer of 1 Kings indicates that, up the hill from David's holy city, Solomon (David's son and successor) built **the first temple of Jerusalem**. It is SACRED STRUCTURE. Then and now, a temple's hallowed halls can mediate God for the faithful. Inside of Solomon's temple, the revered items of the ark and the tablets were given an inner-sanctum home in a room known as the **Holy of Holies.** It was considered so holy that only the high priest could enter it—and he only once a year! On each side of the ark stood winged bronze creatures. The two were called the seraphim. It was believed that God dwelt in this room, hovering over the ark and resting holy feet on the seraphim.

The God for the Israelites of this time, then, is the invisible one residing in the Holy of Holies of Solomon's temple in the city of Jerusalem.

To this general picture we need to add the HOLY OFFICE of the **temple priest**. The priest was considered as mediator of God too. According to ancient tradition, the priestly office was initiated in the Sinai Desert by Moses through his brother Aaron and came, by extension, to those of Aaron's tribe, the **Levites**. The priests shared sacral significance with the king. Priests and king, then, stand between God and the people. There is contemporary evidence of the business of vesting certain people with divine intervention powers as when a minister is called a "Holy Joe" and requested, however lightheartedly, to do something about the weather!

When, after Solomon, the nation split into north and south, the northern tribes reclaimed **Shechem, Bethel,** and **Dan** as their holy shrines. It was my privilege on a trip to Israel several years ago to visit the archaeological dig at Dan and see the "altar of sacrifice." I was somewhat surprised to learn that Yahweh, the God of Moses, was really worshipped there, but that other deities of Canaanite or Phoenician tradition were also honored. Southerners, people living in Jerusalem and Judah, did not accept the northern sacred sites as valid for worship of Yahweh, especially when the priests included the god Baal or the goddess Astarte in their acts of devotion.

Thundering *against* foreign gods and goddesses and *for* ethical righteousness at these northern kingdom sites were the **prophets** Amos and Hosea. Theirs was a HOLY OFFICE too, which enabled them to be spokespersons for God. Hosea said,

> Hear the word of Yahweh, O people of Israel;
>   for Yahweh has an indictment against the inhabitants of the land.
> There is no faithfulness or loyalty,
>   and no knowledge of God in the land.

Hos. 4:1

Amos declared,

> Hear, and testify against the house of Jacob,

says the Lord G<small>OD</small>, the God of hosts:
On the day I punish Israel [the northern kingdom] for its transgressions,
    I will punish the altars of Bethel,
and the horns of the altar shall be cut off
    and fall to the ground.

Amos 3:13–14

Voice for the prophets Amos and Hosea in the 700s BCE, along with that for Micah and Isaiah, was found because they possessed a larger CON-CEPT of God. **Monotheism**, described earlier, was now emerging fully. The prophets understood Yahweh to be the God of *all* people, not just of the Israelites. Speaking for Yahweh, Isaiah called fearsome Assyria "the rod of *my* anger" (Isa. 10:5). This is not henotheism, much less polytheism.

Radical monotheism was coming to Israel and, with it, high ethical demands. The prophets said that Yahweh was a **God of justice and righteousness**. Therefore, when the demands for right social relations are not met, when the widow, the orphan, and the sojourner in your midst are not cared for, the people should know that God's judgment will follow. The ATTRIBUTE of God focused on at this time, then, is God's **righteous anger**. Such anger, the prophets held, would be provoked if Israel did not "do justice, love kindness, and walk humbly with God" (Mic. 6:8). Right-ness needs to be done and will be done, Israel always affirmed. To the point, the words of a contemporary, Martin Luther King Jr., are accurate: "The arc of a moral universe is long, but it bends toward justice."

One person who well understood the meaning of God's requirements was King Josiah. In the year 621 BCE, searching around in the temple, Josiah's priests found a lost manuscript containing laws of Yahweh, laws that were not being followed. He reinstituted those laws in what is called Josiah's reform. The manuscripts discovered are attributed to a writer known as D or the Deuteronomist. The books of the Older Testament in which the writer's hand shows most strongly are Deuteronomy, Joshua, Judges, Samuel, and Kings. The Deuteronomist pulled together Israel's history with Yahweh, casting all that had gone before—from the time of Abraham till his own time—into a framework of meaning. Above all else, he said Yahweh desired a **single king** (Davidic), in **one city** (Jerusalem), with **only the temple** (Solomon's) used for the worship of the **singular God** (Yahweh). All other kings, cities, temples, or gods were not acceptable, as they could not rightly mediate the Holy, so far as the D was concerned.

What prompted Josiah and company to assemble an early Bible was reflection on **the fall of the northern kingdom (Israel) in 722 BCE.**

They interpreted the tragedy as an EVENT revealing God's righteous judgment. Miraculously, Jerusalem, its temple, and the Davidic-line kingship survived the Assyrians, and all were still in tact through the seventh century BCE. The people in Josiah's time hoped that they were staying faithful to Yahweh and therefore would receive Yahweh's protection. In 586, though, their hopes were shattered. **Jerusalem fell** to the Babylonians. Temple and city were destroyed, and the leading citizens (king, priests, prophets, and others) were carried off into captivity, eight hundred miles to the east, to the rivers of Babylon.

The ten northern tribes were now "lost," and Judah of the south lay in ruins, its people deported. The disasters, though, were given theological meaning by the remnant people in exile. Their sufferings were understood as divine judgment. Note, though, they did not interpret this tragedy as God's direct doing but as something *God let happen*, as in "consequences." By the rivers of Babylon the exiled cried out to God. There was much grief, as reflected in the Psalms and the book of Lamentations. Their times and circumstances, though, were viewed as an occasion for **God's faithfulness** to be revealed, if God so chose. They hoped one day to be returned from exile, restored, and made whole again. It may seem strange to give theological meaning to EVENTS NEGATIVE, but that is what our faithparents did. We might remember, even for ourselves, how meaning and significance—even God—come to us on the occasions of *the dark night of the soul*. Out of a church fire, a death, a plant closing, even September 11, 2001, a drawing closer to God can take place. Things seem devastating, but they create a great need for God and open us to a more faithful future. So Israel came to view the destruction of its temple, city, and nation. They waited on God with hope.

The prophet Jeremiah closes this period of our faith history. He talked about a **new covenant** between Yahweh and people, one written on the heart (see Jer. 31:31–34). Jeremiah's understanding began to move God's mediation from "out there" in outward symbol (king, city, temple, and priest) to "in here" for both individual and collective ownership. The new covenant is not a privatistic covenant, as it is made with the people as a whole.

Second Temple Period (550–20 BCE)

(During this time God as Word and Wisdom are emphasized, and a greater understanding of God's universal commitments is lifted.)

"Comfort, O comfort my people," begins the 40th chapter of the book of Isaiah. "Speak tenderly to Jerusalem, and cry to her that she has served her term." What had happened for "comfort" to the people of Israel was **release from captivity–return to Jerusalem**, an EVENT which our faith history celebrates. Cyrus, king of Persia, defeated the Babylonians and then permitted the return of the Jews to their homeland. Captive in Babylon for almost fifty years, the exiles from Judah and Jerusalem were allowed to go home in 538 BCE. They were redeemed, as the captives saw things, and, so, they were given to an understanding that **God is Redeemer**. God was redeemer through a human agent, in this case: Cyrus, whom the Bible calls "**messiah**," that was, one anointed by God. As anointed by God, Cyrus too was, in essence, a HOLY PERSON who mediated God's will and essential character.

So it was that many persons in exile came back to Jerusalem. Also returning was the need for connecting links to God. Over the next 150 years in Jerusalem, there was restoration of the **temple** (albeit less grand), **priests** (more central) to preside in the temple and offer sacrifices, and the **law** (more stringent) à la Ezra. Restoration of Jerusalem, the holy city, is signaled when a new wall goes up around the city.

Many Jews, as they now may be called, did not return to Jerusalem. They stayed in Babylon, spread east to Persia, and went west as far as Spain. In these sundry locations people of the Diaspora planted fig trees, established homes, and sought the welfare of the cities where they lived. So a major reorientation of the faith began *away* from Jerusalem. In new locations they learned new ways of practicing their religion and new things about God. Especially they grasped *what God was not*. They realized God was *not* a deity bound to a particular place or office or object, but one who transcends much of what had previously been understood as necessary for salvation. They affirmed that God may be found, not just in Jerusalem, but in Alexandria, Susa, Corinth, and Rome. A stronger sense of God's **universalism** emerged. The writers of the Bible books of Ruth and Jonah, certainly, had a vision of the wideness in God's mercy. And, as much as anything, Jews discovered that wherever they went, they could have the Law and the Prophets with them. These were rolled in portable scrolls. Further, they could study Torah and worship God in a new mediating institution called **the synagogue**. To be in synagogue on the Sabbath, all they needed was **ten good men** who constituted a quorum and a teacher called a **rabbi**. So in far-flung places the One God with high moral standards was worshipped. In these scattered places, many Gentiles (non-Jews) became interested in this big, ethical God of the Jews. Without being circumcised, these Gentiles attached themselves to the synagogues and became "God-fearers." Quietly, then, the God of Abraham, Isaac, and Jacob was becoming known in the lands of the Medes, Libyans, Greeks, Etruscans, and others.

During these 500 years BCE, with temple-in-Jerusalem and synagogue-in-the-Diaspora, much of the character of the Judaism of Jesus' day took shape. HOLY DAYS came onto the calendar, days that, when kept, mediated the divine: **Rosh Hashanah** (New Year), **Yom Kippur** (Day of Atonement), **Sukkoth** (Booths), **Purim** (Lots), **Pesach** (Passover), and **Shavuot** (Harvest, cf. Pentecost). Above all, **Shabbat** (the seventh day) was honored. Shabbat significance is seen in the opening story of the book of Genesis. Borrowing from an old Babylonian creation story or some other material, the Priestly (P) contributor to the Older Testament described God as creating the world in seven days. He put that account at the beginning of the Scripture and said that on the seventh day God rested. By implication, if you want to be with God, you will rest with God on Shabbat. God is mediated by that day. In time Jews would say, "We do not keep the Sabbath; it keeps us!"

As much as anything else, the Genesis creation story interpreted God as **Creator** of all things, an ATTRIBUTE of God that stays central in our faith to the present day. And let us observe too that creation is by **the Word**. "God **said**, 'Let there be light'; and there was light" (Gen. 1:3). Here and throughout the Scripture, God is presented as the one who speaks *through the prophets*, as historic creeds of the church put it. The Word that is of God is more than past written-down law and prophetic recording. It is lively speech on the tongues of men and women trying to address the world on God's behalf. Today's preacher both reads the Word (of Scripture) aloud and preaches the Word (for the heard utterance).

This understanding of God and Word is "of old" in the tradition. New aspects of God, though, came into being during the years when our faith-parents were ruled by the Persians, 539–333 BCE. Persian culture and ideas entered into thought of Jews in Jerusalem and those in the Diaspora. In particular, Persian Zoroastrianism, with its dualistic interpretation of reality, led people more and more to speak about **the cosmic forces of good vs. the cosmic forces of evil**. In Bible literature now appears talk about a fallen angel, Satan, and hierarchies of angels. There will be images of heaven and hell, as well as belief in a bodily resurrection. All this has origin within Persian culture. Evidence of such influence is found in the book of Job (where Satan talks to God), in Ezekiel (where dry bones are resurrected), and in the extracanonical book of Tobit (where the archangel Raphael is active).

In 333 BCE, the influencing cultural agent became Greece. Alexander the Great of Macedonia came marching through the Middle East, clear to India, reshaping his conquered societies according to the ideals of Greek culture. The Hebrews were not exempt from this influence. Their concept of God took a more philosophic turn. Previously, in our faith-parents' world, little was done in the way of rational speculation about who God is, in and of God's self. In the world of Plato and Aristotle, though, thoughtful people could not escape such philosophical inquiry. Attempts were made at reconciling Hebrew revelations of God with Greek reasoning about God. One of the major thinkers of this time was Philo of Alexandria. He began to use Greek philosophical language about God, which was very helpful and has lasted through modern times. Philo spoke of God's **essence** (or substance, or *ousia*), which is unknowable, and God's **manifestations** (or energies or activities, or *hypostases*), which can be known. The latter is close to what I have been calling **mediations** and the former to what I mean by God's awesome mystery.

From the juncture of Hebrew thought with Greek philosophy, a major new CONCEPT about God found its way into our faith tradition. It concerns **Wisdom** or **Sophia** (Greek for "Wisdom"). Jewish thinkers began to interpret Sophia as the nature of God, essential in creation. To see the influence of the Sophia idea, consider the books of Proverbs and Ecclesiastes; Psalms 49, 51, and 53; and some apocryphal writings. The writers said that Wisdom is to be sought above all things. So, when seeking, finding, and following in the way of Wisdom, one is walking the way with God.

One aspect of the Greek world that our Hebrew ancestors did *not* adopt was statuary in honor of the Holy. The Greeks and Romans portrayed their gods and goddesses—Zeus/Jupiter, Artemis/Diana, for example—in stone. Such portrayals in Hebraic understanding were idols, and these the second commandment explicitly forbade worshipping. So this aspect of the larger culture was influential in a negative sense. Even so, the Greeks tried to impose their way. A Seleucid Greek king, Antiochus IV Epiphanes, despoiled the temple and treasury in Jerusalem in 165 BCE and put a statue of the god Zeus within the Holy of Holies. This "abomination that desolates" (as Dan. 12:11 called it) provoked the Maccabean revolt. Leading the revolt was Judas the Hammerer, who also came to be seen as **messiah** (anointed) of God.

The success of the Maccabean revolt issued in a hundred years of Jewish self-rule. Eventually, though, internal disputes led to an invitation for the Romans to step into the political scene, and in 63 BCE Pompey took control of Jerusalem. The Romans then dominated the Mediterranean world for half a millennium more. Jews chafed under the over-powering Romans.

Because of Roman domination and its concomitant injustices, Jewish thought turned to **apocalyptic ("last things") visions**. Such visions expressed less hope in human work to change things for the better and greater reliance on heavenly deliverance. An "It's-up-to-you-God" mentality was strong. Hope for divine intervention is reflected in Third Isaiah (chapters 56–66), Ezekiel, Joel, and Daniel. In such books we find dreams of another Hammerer, Cyrus, or David—a messiah who would deliver Israel and reestablish God's rule and presence on earth.

Newer Testament Times (20 BCE–110 CE)

(In this time the mediation of God is through Jesus Christ, the Holy Spirit, and the institution(s) of the church.)

Enter now **Jesus of Nazareth**, a PERSON born of woman, raised in a small village in the province of Galilee of Palestine, baptized in the water of the Jordan River, who became a healer and a teacher and . . . *The* **Mediator** between God and humans. He began to be perceived by those who followed him as God's anointed, "Messiah" in Hebrew, "Christ" in Greek. Jesus' followers came to conclude,

> *If you want to know*
> *who or what God is like,*
> *look to Jesus.*

This Jesus, to use the language of Alfred North Whitehead, turns out to be not "the supreme anomaly" among men and women but "the chief exemplification" of what humans are to be and what God is like. We can use hundreds of names to describe Jesus, but one of the earliest names used will suffice for now: Emmanuel, that is, "God with us." (For a fuller treatment of Jesus, see part 3 of this book.)

At the very least, the carpenter from Galilee was a teacher about God and a pointer to God. He came saying that **"God is love"** and that God may be addressed as *"Abba,"* which translates rather closer to "loving daddy" than to "stern father" (see Mark 14:36). This was the God whom Jesus wanted to make known. Jesus spoke often of the Basileia (kingdom, reign, or realm of God, "God's New Order") where the greatest quality of relationships among people would come to be. He proclaimed it and lived it.

Jesus' message and actions were not, however, universally welcomed. He upset pious Pharisees by healing on the Sabbath. He offended social elites by eating with the least and the lost. He angered Sadducee priests by driving money changers from the temple in Jerusalem. So it was that, finally, he was arrested, tried on charges of blasphemy (a religious offense) and sedition (a civil crime), convicted, whipped, and crucified. On a Roman cross he died. He was buried in a borrowed tomb.

The last word on and about Jesus of Nazareth, however, had not been spoken. The mysterious and loving God had a surprise for the world—a surprise that for us is the God EVENT of all time: **the resurrection of Jesus Christ**. When Jesus' sorrowing followers, most notably Mary Magdalene and some other women, came to the tomb to anoint his decaying body with fragrances, they found the tomb empty. Jesus was not there. God had raised him from the tomb in a new spiritual body by which he was revealed to Mary and, then, to others. He became "the risen Christ."

After Jesus' resurrection and postresurrection appearances, his followers struggled to say with words what the meaning of the man Jesus was in relation to God. The apostle Paul says, "*God was in Christ reconciling the world to himself*" (2 Cor. 5:19 mg.). Mark, author of the earliest-written Gospel, says that Jesus is "beloved Son" of God (Mark 1:11 mg. and 9:7 mg.). That word "Son" will make for major new understandings of God. The evangelist John says in 1:14 that the Word (Greek *Logos*) that had been present with God in the beginning "became flesh," incarnate. Stephen Neill in his book *The Many Faces of Christ* notes how each of the Newer Testament writers has a different "take" on Jesus as the Christ. All, though, would agree with Anglican bishop James Robinson when he said that Jesus reveals "the human face of God." As man, **the Human One**, he becomes an incomparably rich and varied symbol of God's fullness.

To the revelation of God in Christ Jesus, the Son, comes a second EXPERIENCE of the early faith community that provides further insight into God. Following Jesus' resurrection appearances and ascension (see Acts 1), his followers were gathered on the day of Pentecost and received "the gift of **the Holy Spirit**." In Acts 2 the experience of the Spirit is described as like the fire of God's presence upon and within them, which enabled them to speak in foreign tongues. They were in-*spired*, even as the prophets of old had been. Under such inspiration the followers of Jesus went out *into all the world* and discovered that the Spirit led them, being especially present at baptism. This understanding of God as Spirit goes back into the Older Testament with the spirit/wind/*ruach* blowing over the face of the water at the time of creation. The Holy Spirit of God is an immensely important way that God was mediated in the first century CE. In Christian interpretation, the Holy Spirit and modern-day "spirituality" are related. (For more conversation on the Spirit's trajectory, see this book's part 4.)

The Holy Spirit gives new dimension to God that will be defined in the centuries ahead under the heading of the Trinity. Suffice to say here that, if God as Father is "above," creating, and as Son is "beside" us, redeeming, then God as Holy Spirit is more "within," sustaining all things.

Son and Spirit, then, are the main mediators for God that we find coming from this time. There are, though, other ways in which God's presence was made available to believers. Early on in the first century, Christians began to worship on Sunday, the first day of the week, the day of Christ's resurrection, rather than on the Sabbath. **Sunday** became a HOLY DAY. People of the Way met to greet the sun, sing praises to God, and partake of a holy meal. That meal usually was of bread and wine, SACRAL FOOD, symbols of the body and blood of Christ broken and poured for them. This meal, called **Holy Communion**, was understood as "a means of grace," a way for connection with God, a mediation.

By partaking of the elements and by being together, Christians of the apostolic age began to see themselves as the body of Christ, also known as **holy church.** Jesus had said, "For where two or three are gathered in my name, I am there among them" (Matt. 18:20). So, the assembly (*ecclesia* in Greek), the church, the body of believers, may also be understood as an INSTITUTION mediating God. During these formative years, believers also instituted a RITE that Jesus had urged upon them, the rite of **baptism.** So, with water, Jesus' followers were sealed as they entered the faith. Baptism, especially baptism by immersion, was a rich symbol of cleansing, of dying and being reborn in Christ, signaling a new relationship with God.

In this period, then, the PERSON of **Jesus as the Christ**, the EXPERIENCE of **the Holy Spirit**, and the INSTITUTION of **the church** with its SACRED RITES of **baptism** and **Holy Communion** were, then, some of the "means" by which men and women grew into love and knowledge of God. Two thousand years later, these "things" still mediate.

Chapter Five

God in the Early Church

Struggling Centuries of the Church (110-500 CE)

(In this period "Jesus is Lord" begins creedal confessions leading into the doctrine of the Trinity; other mediations develop, such as the scriptural canon.)

The first three centuries of the Christian church were difficult ones indeed. The church was growing, spreading out in the Roman Empire (and beyond). Our religion, a branch of the religion of ancient Israel, was not easily understood or appreciated by imperial Roman authorities. For one thing, Christians refused to bend the knee to anyone but God, certainly not to Caesar. For another thing, they refused to serve in the army and would not attend Coliseum events. Beginning as early as 64 CE and continuing intermittently till the beginning of the fourth century, the Romans persecuted Christians. Many became **martyrs**, special "witnesses" for the faith.

Those who suffered martyrdom often did so with three words on their lips: **"Jesus is Lord."** Those three words were the earliest confession of faith. They are found in the Newer Testament when the apostle Peter makes his great confession, saying to Jesus, "You are the Messiah [the Christ], the Son of the living God" (Matt. 16:16). Martha of Bethany made the same confession in John 11:27. A fuller statement of faith is in Paul's letter to the church at Philippi, chapter 2, verses 5–11, ending with the words that "every tongue should confess that Jesus Christ is Lord, to the glory of God the Father." So for the early church, "Jesus is Lord" is a fresh and substantive statement about the man Jesus and God.

A second formulation is suggested to Christians in the last verses of the Gospel of Matthew, where Jesus says, "Go therefore and make disciples of all nations, baptizing them in the name of the Father and of the Son and of the Holy Spirit" (Matt. 28:19). We have in this phrase an incipient doctrine of **the Trinity**. The word *Trinity* was first used by Tertullian of North Africa in the late second century. He may have been stimulated to create it after hearing the Apostles' Creed, dated from the year 150 CE. The creed has a threefold structure to it, affirming faith in God as (1) **Father**, (2) **Son**, and (3) **Holy Ghost** or **Holy Spirit**. Despite the threeness presented, God is still *one* God. As Tertullian tried to explain, the Trinity was "one God in three Persons," that is, having three *personae* "masks" behind which the same essential Being exists. If the reader is puzzled here, that is understandable, for the doctrine of the Trinity is, finally, "a mystery." It can be presented oversimplistically with the analogy of H_2O, which takes three forms: water, ice, and steam. This analogy fails to explain the Trinity and is officially a Christian heresy, but it is suggestively helpful.

A more careful articulation of faith in the **triune God** had to wait for a time when leadership of the churches could gather and consult. Such a time finally came through a Roman general named Constantine. Raised by a Christian mother but not a Christian himself, Constantine saw a sign of Christ in the clouds just before he went into a critical battle. He won the battle and, in a few years' time, gained control of the whole Roman Empire, becoming its emperor. Favoring Christians, he invited bishops from all over the empire to gather in Nicaea (near his soon to be new imperial capital in Constantinople) and make decisions as a body about the church, especially on doctrine. The bishops gathered for what is known as the **First Ecumenical** COUNCIL. I here capitalize Council, for this council and the six after it determine articulations of truth(s) about God for the people of God. At Nicaea the council formulated Christianity's first official statement of orthodoxy: the **Nicene Creed.** This CREED has mediated an understanding of God's nature for billions of Christians over the centuries.

At the time of the drafting of the Nicene Creed, there was widespread controversy about the relation of the Son to the Father. One Arius of Alexandria said that "there was a time when the Son was not" and only the Father existed. Bishop Athanasius, also of Alexandria, held that the Father and Son were together, the *same*, at the beginning. Athanasius's perspective prevailed at Nicaea and became "orthodox" belief. His work was augmented and refined by theologians of Cappadocia (in today's central Turkey). In formulating doctrine they relied on the Greek philosophic distinction between

God's *ousia* (essential nature, which is unknowable, divine mystery)
and
God's *hypostases* (energies or powers, which are knowable).

We had seen something of this idea in the writings of Philo four centuries earlier. Here the Cappadocians said that God's *hypostases* were like facial expressions that hinted at God's inner nature, though the fullness of God in God's deepest self is never fully known.[1]

Not all theological issues were clarified at Nicaea. Subsequent councils were called, such as the Council of Constantinople in 381 and one in Ephesus in 431. At the Fourth Ecumenical Council, in Chalcedon in 451, a strong declaration was made about the two natures of Christ, that he was *truly God and truly man . . . in two natures without confusion, without change, without division, without separation.*

The theological writer held in highest regard—at least in the West—for his reflections on God is Augustine of Hippo, bishop in North Africa. His *On the Trinity* describes the Godhead as the mind with (1) knowledge, (2) reason, and (3) will, yet still one mind. Augustine also develops the thought of Paul to the effect that what mediates God to humanity is God's **grace,** freely given through Christ, and received in **faith** by humans. Grace and faith, like love, are SACRED EXPERIENCES. While grace, love, and faith are not physical entities, they are nevertheless real, part of our heart and mind and emotions, all experienced in the material body. Augustine said, "O Lord, thou hast made us for thyself, so our **hearts** are restless till they rest in thee."

Other, more concrete mediations for this period may be noted. Consider the **Bible,** so important to the people of Israel and, likewise, to Christians. By the time of Jesus in the first century CE, most of the writings that made up the Older Testament were in circulation. These, though, were loose documents until 90 CE. In that year rabbis meeting in Jamnia (coastline of west Judea), decided which books would be and which books would not be in their CANON of sacred writings, which included Law, Prophets, and Writings. Christians continued to hold these books sacred too, but various locales of the church accepted other books found in the Greek or Septuagint (LXX) version of the Bible. They are in some modern Bibles under the heading of the Apocrypha or deutero-canonical books. For all persons—whatever the exact makeup of books—the **Older Testament** functioned as window into God.

At the Council of Jamnia, besides deciding on the sacred canon, the rabbis effectively expelled believers in Jesus from synagogues. We can date the separation of rabbinic Judaism and Christian Judaism (Christianity) from that date. Part of the dispute between the two branches had to do with writings that the followers of Christ held sacred but that rabbinic Jews would not so regard: the letters of Paul and others, the Gospels, Acts, and Revelation. These circulated among the churches and, more and more, took on sacred status. There was dispute, though, about what writings were "of God." The question was finally settled in the fourth century, partially at Nicaea, when Constantine ordered that authoritative Christian writings be assembled. The collection included our current twenty-seven books. In the year 367, Athanasius in a *Festal Letter* identified the same twenty-seven books as Christian Scripture. Thus the **Newer Testament** came to be. Insofar as it is the cradle in which Christ is rocked, it is the incomparable mediation to God, our inspiration and our source of revelation.

I have described these centuries-after-Jesus as "struggling" years, in that the followers of Jesus struggled to spread the gospel in the world, survive persecution, define themselves in the world of Greek and Roman thought, and get their organizational house in order. Most of these struggles were over by the early fifth century. Christianity was remarkably ensconced, and its understanding of God widely agreed upon.

The Age of Monasticism (500–1100 CE)

(In this period many "practices" of Christians become mediations to and for God; Christ becomes distant, and the Blessed Virgin Mary functions more and more as a mediator.)

Persecution of Christians by the Romans in the early centuries of the church meant that there was suffering for the faith, sometimes martyrdom. After persecution ended and the church moved into a preferential situation, there were devotees who would have no soft life in the now-accepting Greco-Roman world. These men and women opted to do sacrificial identification with Christ. Their way was through the RELIGIOUS LIFE of **monasticism**. Some monks went off into the desert to meet God in **ascetic aloneness**. Others became part of gathered communities where poverty, chastity, and obedience were practiced and ***ora et labora*** ("pray and work") was the order of their days. The monasteries and convents kept faith and learning alive during the centuries of invasion and occupation by the German tribes and, later, the Vikings.

For the monasteries and convents in the eastern part of the Roman Empire, Basil of Caesarea had given general rules for communal life. In the West, Benedict of Nursia provided a more detailed rule. In the monasteries east and west, during the second half of the first millennium great devotional service to God occurred. An eastern monk named Dionysius the Pseudo-Areopagite (ca. 500 CE) wrote *Mystical Theology*, in which he described "ways" of the spiritual life, to include (1) **purgation**, (2) **illumination**, and (3) **union**. He spoke about a process of "**unknowing**" in which the mind and senses were quieted, that the believer might be opened to the coming of God's Spirit.

In the West, Duns Scotus Erigena (d. 877), a monk cloistered in Paris, translated Dionysius's work and offered his own theological contribution. He held that God, animating the created world, also reveals God's self in **flowers, birds, trees, and human beings**. Erigena's thinking is very Irish (he was a Celt) and somewhat pantheistic. Another great mind of these centuries was that of Anselm of Canterbury (d. 1109). He offered a definition of God still helpful to many people: "something, than which no greater can be thought." This statement emphasizes the **mind and thought** as the way to approach, even "prove" God. Anselm, though, always held that faith (first) is pursuing understanding. "I believe in order to understand," he says.

Anselm is also remembered for his theory of atonement (how we are made at one with God). He understood that God's majesty has been dishonored by human sin, and that no mortal could overcome the offense. But then God himself through Jesus offered up an acceptable sacrifice, effecting God's acceptance of humanity. Anselm's God was a **stern moralist**. Increasingly through the years, Christ came to be seen as ascended to heaven, where he reigns with God the Father and has become a **demanding judge**. In the Eastern or Greek Orthodox Church a similar conception of the deity is conveyed on the dome ceilings of churches. There is the **Pantocrator** (Ruler of All), with one hand holding a book of names and the other hand having fingers slightly raised to suggest, "Is your name here?" God and Jesus were becoming hard and distant in many a believer's imagination.

The severe picture of divinity was counterbalanced by popular devotion to Mary the Mother of Jesus, venerated as ***Theotokos,*** meaning "God-Bearer." The Virgin Mary came to be a major mediator of God for people, giving the holy God compassion. To the current day, Mary's star has set neither in the East among Orthodoxy nor in the West among Catholics. The Madonna (with or without child) is doubtless the most painted and sculpted subject in the world. In the Eastern Orthodox Church, the Theotokos shares a center position with Christ on the doors to the inner sanctum. **Icons** of Mary and Jesus are there to be kissed and venerated, enabling mediation of God. Faithful worshippers are convinced the icons connect them to the Holy.

Icon use in churches was challenged during the eighth century, though, in the iconoclastic controversy. Emperor Leo III wanted to purify the church and get rid of art that seemed to be graven images. His concern for icon removal was response to the seventh-century rise of Islam, a strong monotheistic religion with zero tolerance for icons. Islam seemed to the emperor a judgment of God against Christians for their lack of obedience to the second commandment. Monks, priests, and people, though, wanted to keep the icons. A fight over icons lasted for a hundred years until a new imperial ruler relented, and **icons** were returned for veneration. Their importance continues to the present day.

For Emperor Leo and others, the **rise of Islam** was a negative EVENT, like the destruction of Jerusalem in 586 BCE, that revealed God in God's anger. In a more positive interpretation, Islam's coming was a chastening experience for Christians, causing a reexamination of essentials, including the understanding of God. The fact that Islam was a radical monotheism worked on Christians to reemphasize God's oneness over God's threeness in the Trinity. Meanwhile, though, Islamic armies conquered traditional Christian strongholds, from Persia through North Africa to Spain.

Nevertheless, Christianity found an opening for growth to the north. Missionaries from Ireland went into Scotland and areas where Germanic tribes earlier had overrun Christian boundaries. Monks from France moved north into Germany and, eventually, into the Scandinavian countries, trying to convert pagan Vikings who in the ninth and tenth centuries plundered western and eastern (Russian) Europe. Theologically the situation was like the Older Testament competition of Elijah with the prophets of Baal, but here the contest was between monks like Boniface or Anskar and the priests of Woden and Odin. Christ eventually prevailed.

In the East during the 800s, the Orthodox Christian monks, Cyril and Methodius, introduced Christianity to Slavic peoples. Bulgar people also became Christians. Finally, the faith came to Russia in the year 988 CE, when Tsar Vladimir was baptized. In time, the Russians would declare their PLACE, **Moscow**, to be the Third Rome, superceding Constantinople, the Second Rome.

Meanwhile Charlemagne in France was starting to reunite Europe into a new world order, the Holy Roman Empire. Crowned Emperor in 800 CE, Charlemagne worked out mutual support arrangements with Pope

Leo III. So began centuries of church and state collaboration as well as competition. Charlemagne's successors were especially supportive of monasticism, specifically the monastery in Cluny, France. It became the motherhouse for more than a thousand organized chapter monasteries across Europe. At Cluny monks built one of the largest churches in the Christian world, a structure 555 feet long. They engaged in liturgical renewal and powerful **chant singing**. They encouraged scholarship and manuscript copying, provided social services to their nearby communities, and much more, helping to ameliorate and close the Dark Ages.

What needs to be reiterated is that **monasteries** and **convents,** in a very rough world, provided SACRED PLACES (like **Cluny**) and HOLY PERSONS (**monks** and **nuns**) with an alternative vision of society in which God could come nearer. Monasticism supplied the missionaries, carried culture and learning, provided human services, and kept the faith alive and well, providing an avenue to God (mediation) for people. This was done through SPIRITUAL PRACTICES followed and modeled, to wit: **fasting, living simply, pilgrimages, honoring the saints, venerating relics, celibacy, chanting**, and, above all else, **praying.** In these ways, then, Christians of late antiquity lived with God, believing that, upon their death, they would enter heaven with God and the saints.

High Christendom Years (1100–1450 CE)

(In this period the sacramental system of Catholicism is established and Thomas Aquinas's ideas of God are adopted.)

It was long asserted by the Catholic Church in Rome that the first pope, Peter, had received from Christ the "keys to the kingdom." Many Western Christians believed that whoever Peter and his successor popes bound or loosed on earth would be bound or loosed in heaven (see Matt. 16:19). Through this tradition, **the Roman Catholic Church,** itself an INSTITUTION, became a means of mediating God. Doctrine was established that *there is no salvation outside the church*, and faithful Catholics believed it. So long as the believers were in the grace of the church, they were *ipso facto* connected to God. This may sound strange to contemporary people, but, as noted at the beginning of these chapters, times and circumstances were different.

The church as mediator inherited and devised other mediations in its sacramental system or HOLY RITES. These were what really helped the faithful. Seven sacraments—**baptism, confession, communion, confirmation, marriage, holy orders,** and **last rites**—were fixed as basic in the

Roman church. They are in effect today. Their purpose was to save people's souls and keep them in a state of grace that they might avoid hell and go to heaven. What the reader might note is that **heaven** and **hell** are CONCEPTUALIZATIONS that bespeak eternal destiny, if not the eternal Judge. The hereafter had power. So people could reason, "God is up in heaven watching me, surrounded by my departed loved ones, who are expecting me to arrive; therefore, I'd better believe, act morally, and observe holy sacraments while on earth."

In the medieval world, everything was hierarchical. Class lines were clear and inflexible. Institutions (governmental, military, church, guilds) had someone at the top, with others arranged in tiers below. In the **hierarchy of being**, over and above all was God. Below God were archangels and angels (who became immensely important in this period); then came humans. In the feudal system, there were the nobility, artisans, and peasants. In the hierarchy, men were over women and, below them, children. Animals were next on the chain of being.

There was also hierarchy in cosmology. Above was heaven (to which believers aspired), in the middle was earth, and beneath was hell (which was feared). Hell had layers too, such as limbo (where unbaptized babies went), purgatory (for punishment), and the lowest realm (for the totally unredeemable). Already in popular imagination, heaven and hell were described in the fourteenth-century writings of Dante, his most popular piece called *The Inferno*. Escape from hell was provided people in the West by the sacramental system over which the church in Rome had control.

A story from the eleventh century illustrates the power of Roman Catholicism and its sacramental system. When King Henry IV of Germany interfered with church reform in 1077, Pope Gregory VII put the king and his subjects under an interdict, which included withholding of the sacraments from people in Henry's realm. The interdict alarmed people greatly and thus threatened the position of the monarch with his subjects. Henry knew he had to make things right with the church and get the interdict lifted. So he came to Italy over the Alps barefooted in winter and humbled himself for three days in the rain and cold at the pope's door. Finally he was granted an audience and absolved from his sins, thus lifting the interdict. The church had power.

Power was there but power, we know, often corrupts. Pope Urban II launched a Holy War in 1095 to stop the advance of the Seljuk Turks on Christian Byzantium and also to capture the traditional holy lands for Western Christianity. For two centuries Christians and Muslims fought. To all who would fight, the church granted forgiveness of all sins, past, present, and future! This blanket absolution, called an **indulgence**, was later offered for monetary purchase to ordinary citizens. The purchase enabled souls in purgatory to have their way paid out. Later reformers would object to indulgences and to the system behind them. The point is that at this time God was perceived as up in heaven, and the church had the means to get the faithful up there.

"Up" was better, and the ARCHITECTURE of the time reflected such a notion. **Great Gothic cathedrals** were built all over Europe with skyline-dominating spires pointing to God. These churches did much to mediate God through their beauty, their high holy **masses** (often sung), and their storytelling ART of **stained-glass windows, carvings, mosaics,** and **paintings**. The message was carried too by **morality plays** enacted in church yards and city squares.

It should be noted that there was significant theological underpinning to the church's worldview and mediation practices. Such underpinning was provided by the great universities that sprang up within the shadow of the cathedrals of Europe. Here scholars pondered theological questions. They believed MIND to be a category for mediation. The great intellect of Thomas Aquinas at the University of Paris reworked the writings of the ancient philosopher Aristotle for Christian compatibility. Like Anselm before him, Aquinas believed "faith leads to understanding." Faith led, Aquinas believed, to where **reason and natural law** could be "enlightening unto God." In his *Summa Theologicae*, Aquinas offered faith-based proofs for the existence of God, describing God as the **Unmoved Mover** and **First Cause.** In the hierarchal scheme of things Aquinas suggested that faithful believers might "work" their way toward God.

Theologians notwithstanding, others followed not an intellectual way to God but a MYSTICAL route. The face of God, so far as Hildegard of Bingen (d. 1179), Meister Eckhart (d. 1327), and others were concerned, was to be seen through the disciplined life of **contemplative prayer** and other spiritual practices. The unknown author of the fourteenth-century book *The Cloud of Unknowing* recommended such prayer, which involves clearing of all "thought" and breathing a holy name, such as "God" or "Love" as the way to know God. It involved the practitioner in being open to the Spirit, which Hildegard described in a poem:

> The Holy Spirit is life that gives life
> Moving all things.
> It is the root of every creature,
> And purifier of all things,

Wiping away sins,
Anointing wounds.
It is radiant life, worthy of praise,
Awakening and enlivening all things.[2]

Other religious persons seemed to find God neither by the intellectual way nor by contemplation but by living simple lives of **poverty, chastity, and obedience**. Such living now, though, was in the world, not in cloistered communities. Men and women of faith would be on the streets, serving people, even lepers. Francis of Assisi and Sister Clare lived such humble lives and established the "Little Brothers" and "Poor Clares" orders, into which many other persons came. For them, the face of God was to be seen in **the poor, sick, and suffering** of the earth, just as Jesus had said.

In much of the above, it was **works,** the moral efforts of men and women, that were believed able to lead to God. Some, though, such as John Wycliffe and John Huss, began to question the "good works" orientation. Their voices could not be well *heard*, however, because their words could not be *seen*. Invisibility of word would change with the invention of movable type for a printing press in 1456. The printed page would change the world, enabling reformers to be heard—that is, read—effectively and broadly.

Chapter Six

God in the Later Church

Reformations/New Worlds Era (1450–1650 CE)

(In this period God's grace and human faith again become ascendant, the Bible is emphasized, the utter sovereignty of God is affirmed, and the face of God takes on new hues and shapes.)

An Augustinian monk in Wittenberg, Germany, is the person most remembered for redirecting thought about God. His name? Martin Luther. The question "What must I do to be saved?" deeply troubled him. The usual answer to such question had been "Do works of righteousness and live purely." Luther, however, found that neither works nor prayer nor mortification of flesh gave him a sense of being justified before God. God seemed the harsh taskmaster who could not be pleased. Luther studied and wrestled his way to an old, almost forgotten conclusion about how humans are saved and about the God who is active in the saving process. With Paul and Augustine, he said, "We are saved *sola fide*—by faith alone"—and it is faith in the **grace of God.** Instead of seeing God as a severe judge, Luther came to understand God as the loving Other who seeks and saves through Jesus Christ. Humans need only accept God's action and believe. *God,* said Luther in his famous hymn, *is a mighty fortress, a bulwark never failing.* To be in God's mighty fortress, Luther said, we do not have to lay siege and break in. God has already landed us safe inside!

Authority for Luther and other Protestant reformers shifted away from the pope and councils of the church and toward **the Bible.** This SACRED TEXT, Luther believed, mediated God quite sufficiently. Protestants became a people of the Book, and Johannes Gutenburg's invention helped it happen. Luther translated the Newer Testament, and it was soon in print, in German! Luther's sermons and other writing, often polemical, went into circulation too, attracting adherents for his thinking.

As important as the *written* word was for Protestants, the *spoken* word was given special standing. **Preaching** took on new value. Luther recognized only two sacraments (baptism and Communion), but, in effect, he made preaching a third. It was by the Word spoken that God's saving address is most powerfully communicated, Luther said. Subsequent Protestantism has agreed.

Luther was joined in his new thinking by John Calvin in Geneva. Calvin also emphasized grace appropriated by faith, but he put emphasis on the *grace* side which, thereby, lifted up God's **sovereignty**, God's absolute rule. Calvin held that God's rule is for all of life, including the body politic. So the magistrates in Geneva created a **theocracy** (government by God). Belief in the sovereignty of God lent itself to affirmation of predestination (God's knowing and willing what will happen ahead of time), for which the Reformed branch of the church, Calvin's, is often remembered.

A third beachhead for Protestantism occurred in England. King Henry VIII, who had been designated "protector of the faith" by the pope, wanted to gain control of the church in England. He wanted the monastic orders' properties and the pope's prerogative to make rulings on marriage and divorce. That he might get a church-sanctioned divorce, King Henry broke with Rome in 1533 and created the Church of England. This church's Archbishop Cranmer allowed for Henry's divorce and remarriage . . . and remarriages. The new Anglican Church maintained the basic liturgical shape of the Catholic mass with two important changes. First, the liturgy was thenceforth spoken in English; second, an English *Book of Common Prayer* was birthed for use in worship. It became—and is for Anglicans yet—a quite SACRED BOOK.

The fourth wing of the Protestant Reformation was the Anabaptist. The Anabaptists affirmed **adult believers'** baptism, usually by immersion, as RITE to holiness. They also emphasized that humans have free will in relation to God: God is not predetermining all things, as Calvin held. A pastor in Holland by the name of Arminius thought this free-will way and posited a **God who waits in love** for human decisions. Some groups of Anabaptists, like the Mennonites—and later, other Christians, like the Quakers—practiced pacifism, as had the early church. The Quakers also emphasized a new quietism, God as **divine spark** within each person, available in silent attentiveness.

Overall Protestant thought about God returned Christianity to a more biblically based religion and a shedding of accruements of ancient and medieval times. God, formerly high and abstract, became more intimate and involved, less Greek, more Hebraic. There was markedly less mysticism and more rationality—some would say more propositional understanding—about God. The monastic set-apart life was undercut, giving way to emphasis on the local church and the priesthood of all believers, though men were still "more equal" than women. The Virgin Mary was effectively dethroned in Protestant countries, and Christ was reinstalled. Pilgrimages ceased. The use of Latin in worship, along with chanting, disappeared. In place of the clergy or boys chanting, **congregational hymn singing** began, which ever since has had power to enliven God for worshippers. Christianity took on a decidedly different look in northern European climes.

Understandably, Catholic popes and bishops sought to stop the Protestant movement, but prelates recognized validity in some of the Reformers' ideas. To address internal reform and to organize response to Protestantism, the Council of Trent was convened, and during its years, 1545–63, many changes were instituted, such as limitation of indulgence selling. Thomas Aquinas's "medieval synthesis" of thought, which, among other characteristics, held **God as the goal** (*telos*) of all human endeavors, was adopted as normative for Catholics. The Catholic Counter-Reformation was strengthened, especially in outreach, by the Society of Jesus. Jesuits sought to expand the faith (as to China and Japan), to restore intellectual rigor, and to improve devotional life. Founder Ignatius Loyola wrote his *Spiritual Exercises*, giving a new, experiential form of spiritual life.

With strong differences existing between Protestants and Catholics— and among Protestants, as well as differences with Eastern Orthodoxy— conflict leading to violence broke out. War came, the most bloody being the Thirty Years' War, which dislocated and killed hundreds of thousands of people.

By 1650 most Europeans were exhausted from religious zealotry and war. They were open to alternative, even nonreligious, ways of thinking (which science and the Enlightenment, as we shall see in the next section, provided). Escape from war also came via the "discovery" of the new worlds. Into the Americas and into Africa and Asia, explorers and "developers" went. They usually were accompanied by priests and brothers of various orders who became missionary evangelists. God was understood by the missionaries and then presented to native peoples usually as *Christus Victor*, the conquering Christ. This Christ came with imperialism, colonialism, enslavement, plantation life, and European cultural imposition. In the Caribbean and in Central and South America, Christianity was, at one level, forced upon native peoples by the Spanish and Portuguese, but it was also adopted *and adapted*. For native people, two things should be noticed with regard to God. While the conquistadors came under the banner of Christus Victor, what native people saw and experienced was a **suffering God in the crucified Christ,** *Christus Victus* (Victim). This was a God to whom they could relate, who knew exactly the life they knew. Just as important, native people in Central America found solace in a feminine face of God. In 1531 **Our Lady of Guadalupe** was revealed to a Mexican Indian, Juan Diego, and she has been the main mediator for millions ever since.

In the art of native cultures everywhere, God's face in Christ took on more color and contours to be Indian, African, Chinese, and so forth.

Beginning in the early 1600s, Protestant Christians started coming to North America. They came not just to gain wealth or convert native people but to establish new homes for themselves and live in the New World permanently. We in the United States think first of the Pilgrims who landed at Plymouth Rock in 1620 and of the Puritans who quickly followed to make a "New" England. These folk were of Reformed persuasion, seeking, as had Calvin in Geneva, to set up a **New Jerusalem,** as PLACE was still an important category for relating to God.

The Ecumenical Age (1650 CE–Present)

(In this period God moves inward, identified by the subjective "feeling" of dependence, God has more diverse modes of mediation, and unity in God grows.)

Place and other general categories for the mediation of God, like sacred text and rites, in the last several hundred years have given way to AFFECTIONS (emotions, feelings) for the realm of God. Opening for the affections was signaled in the 1600s by Blaise Pascal, who wrote, "The heart has reasons that reason knows not of." It was carried forward into the 1700s with the rise of Pietism, which also believed that God was to be found by **warming within the heart** and less by theologizing with the head. The Moravians, one group of Pietists, were influential on a young Anglican priest, John Wesley, who experienced Moravian praying and singing on a return trip to England from colonial Georgia. Back in London, in a simple religious service one evening, he had a deep religious experience about which he said, "My heart was strangely warmed."

Theological underpinning for Wesley and others' religion of the heart was provided in the early 1800s by German theologian Friedrich Schleiermacher. Writing *Treatises on Religion to Its Cultured Despisers*, he offered a definition of God that made sense to modern people. He said that "religion is the **feeling of absolute dependence** on God." This has different meaning to it than earlier God-talk. The emphasis was on subjectivity, on "feeling," not on thought or objective perception of a Being who is external. God is not so much "out there" as "in here," Schleiermacher suggests, decidedly more immanent than transcendent. When one begins to think of relating to God from the inside, people's religion becomes much more psychological and individualistic, which is a fair description of Schleiermacher's age and ours. To put the best possible Christian interpretation on our time, we should say that recent centuries have been the years of the **Holy Spirit dwelling within.**

Keeping more traditional Christianity in his thought, yet bowing to putting emphasis on the individual was the Danish theologian Søren Kierkegaard. He also was of a mind that subjectivity was the route to God and said that belief in God through Christ was decidedly up to "the solitary individual." That individual, however, was faced with a mind-confusing paradox when encountering the Christian message: the individual was asked to believe that the *eternal* God came to be *in time*. This is a crucifixion of the understanding, Kierkegaard said, which cannot be resolved by greater knowledge but by a **"leap of faith."** The solitary individual, then, is swimming over 30,000 fathoms of water, believing in the virtue of the absurd, to use two of the Dane's favorite expressions. The leap, he believed, would be taken for one's eternal happiness.

Pascal, Wesley, Schleiermacher, and Kierkegaard have had influence right to the present day. I talk about them first in this section because I believe that they described for us what has been the dominant religious PARADIGM of the last several hundred years: **subjective, heartwarming experience** as the touchstone for relating to God. Theologians as sophisticated as Paul Tillich will subscribe to this interpretation, and evangelists like Billy Graham will use it to "win souls to Christ." In the latter part of the twentieth century a variation of subjectivity started sweeping much of Christianity worldwide: Pentecostalism or the charismatic movement. It includes considerable Catholic, Protestant, and new religious movement constituency. Pentecostalism is quite psychological in that tongues-speaking and other ecstatic expressions come from *within* people, who say God has touched them there. God is apprehended less by the Bible and more by the **Holy Spirit working within.** In third-world countries, Pentecostalism has had an immensely popular reception.

The cultural backdrop for much of this redefinition of God and how humans relate to God may be understood in a review of the Age of Reason and the rise of science. In many ways the Christian religion was *against* what these two enormous secular influences presented, but also there was adoption and adaptation to them. The Enlightenment and the scientific worldview were—really are—the movements creating modernity. Both laid emphasis on the inquiring mind to discover and chart individual destiny in a most physical world. Both the Age of Reason and the rise of science had their beginnings in the seventeenth century.

The Age of Reason

The Age of Reason, sometimes called the Enlightenment, was shaped by new thought arising in intellectual circles of Europe. Beginning with René Descartes (d. 1650), we see the importance of mind in his famous Cogito, ergo sum (“**I am thinking**, therefore, I am”). That conclusion about his own existence was followed immediately by Descartes's positing the existence of God. This God was not Christianity's Trinity but abstract unity. Joining Descartes was the Jewish philosopher Baruch Spinoza (d. 1677) in the Netherlands with strong doubt about both the God of traditional Christianity *and* Judaism. He believed that nothing about God could be known or experienced, for God was totally detached from the world. At best, God, like a clockmaker, had made the world, started it running, and then walked away to let it go on its own. More inclusive of God-allowance was Lord Herbert of Cherbury (d. 1648), who was the first deist. Cherbury concluded that all religions have five common ideas: (1) God exists, (2) God must be worshipped, (3) worship should have ethical results, (4) humans have a need to repent, and (5) there is reward-punishment in this life and the next. A little later, John Locke (d. 1704) in England held similarly that the existence of God could be ascertained by natural reason and that God's law, by which we rightly may conduct ourselves, could be known. Other philosophers, notably Voltaire (d. 1778) in France and David Hume (d. 1776) in England came to doubt all they heard of God and became, essentially, atheists. Not an atheist but a deist was Jean-Jacques Rousseau (d. 1778). Rousseau, among the most influential figures in the Age of Reason, affirmed a natural religion in which God had set up a moral universe, such that God made himself available to humans through **conscience**. In discussing conscience, please note, we are back under the heading of individualism in religion.

Enlightenment thinkers (Cherbury, Locke, and Rousseau, especially) had a major impact on the shape of the emerging United States. With the rationalists, the founders of this country rejected the divine right of kings and, before the French Revolution started, called for "liberty, equality, and fraternity." Enlightenment thinking laid the foundation for the American Revolution against England. Conscience (hence, God) told the colonists that bondage needed to be broken. It was.

The new United States, having successfully separated from England and the English religious establishment, set the course for a new structure of church-state relations. The 1789 Constitution and Bill of Rights started to disestablish religion. Churches could no longer rely on the instruments of government to support them. A kind of open market for religion thus began in this country. To survive, churches needed to become evangelical. They supported the idea that there really was **free will** (à la Arminius, the Baptists, and the Methodists), making it incumbent on the individual to decide what he or she believed about God and would do in that relationship. God became **the one calling and awaiting personal decision**.

In this way, the Age of Reason effected the history of religion in America and, if you will, God. By the middle of the nineteenth century rationalism's influence was waning, but it had made great impact, as illustrated by the fact that every American president in his inaugural speech nods to the deistic God.

The Rise of Science

Science is the second major force shaping the modern world, but whereas the first force, rationalism, has faded, science and technology have not ceased from influencing what people believe about God. Through Copernicus (d. 1543), Galileo (d. 1642), Newton (d. 1727), Darwin (d. 1882), and Curie (d. 1934)—to name one scientist per century—we have all been changed materially and in the way we think, even about God. Ostensibly science is concerned only about the physical universe and how it operates. It does not need God as a working hypothesis. When scientists have given thought to God, though, it has been a **God operating by the laws of nature**. Sir Isaac Newton, working out the laws of physics (e.g., gravity), said piously that he was thinking God's thoughts after him. Newton and others thought of a mechanical universe in which natural laws were immutable.

At the turn of the twentieth century a cosmic shift in the scientific community's understanding of "reality" came about. The world, earlier seen as operating by fixed static laws, now needed to make room for mutability. Albert Einstein believed there is relativity in the universe. A physicist-philosopher named Heisenberg spoke of an "uncertainty principle" that makes things not quite so predictable. Still others noticed that randomness happens in the physical ordering of things. Such new thinking, when applied to the religious world, suggested that God would not be bound by unchangeable laws but might be given freedom of action—wiggle room, if you will. **God could be dynamic**, not static, even as the world was increasingly perceived as dynamic. A mathematician turned philosopher, Alfred North Whitehead, appropriated the changes in the scientific worldview and began to write of God as "**in process**." God, world, and humanity were alive, changing, becoming. As it turns out, this unbounded God is more like the God of the Bible than the God of Greek, Thomistic, and Enlightenment philosophers.

Still another take on God from the world of science was birthed in the field of psychology. Sigmund Freud, founder of psychotherapy, got people thinking in new ways about mental and emotional states and processes. Freud held that God was not real in any way but was a projection of humans, a wish fulfillment. Rejecting this interpretation was Carl Jung, who saw in the deep recesses of human consciousness a **collective unconscious**, which he believed was of God. In the collective unconscious, divine archetypal images of a Wise Old Man, a Great Mother figure, and a Divine Child are present. When, then, the Divine Child "within" meets up with the Bambino (Christ child) "without," a religious connection of great personal meaning may be fired. Jung said he did not *believe* there was a God; he *knew* it. Here again, we have a "triumph of the therapeutic" in religion, so that the religious world has moved greatly inward, à la Schleiermacher.

So the rise of science has greatly influenced what we *think* about God.

Many Christians, though, viewed science as a threat to the faith. Galileo was forced by the Catholic Church to deny his agreement with Copernicus that the earth moves around the sun. Publicly he recanted; privately he mumbled, "But it still moves!" Some Christians did not like Lisle's geological theories that the earth was billions of years old, as that thesis did not agree with the Genesis seven-day creation account. And certainly Christians found Charles Darwin's theory on the origin of species by evolution repugnant. So much was this the case that in 1925 a court case in Dayton, Tennessee, called the Scopes Monkey Trial, sought to ban the teaching of evolution in the schools. The antievolution side prevailed, but evolution is the operating assumption today in biology classes nationwide. Most Christians have reconciled themselves with the scientific view on origins, saying that God could just as well have worked by evolution in designing humans as by spontaneous generation. For Christians, God's eternity just got longer, and God is the **author of evolution**.

Antievolution thinkers did not agree with such liberal interpretations of God and the Bible. These conservatives thought that such biblical accounts as Joshua's stopping the sun or Jesus' walking on the water should not be disbelieved just because these things were not duplicable by scientists in a laboratory. Their view came out of what is called *fundamentalist* Christianity which holds to a literal interpretation of the Bible. They say the Scriptures are divinely inspired and, therefore, inerrant. One fundamentalist preacher proclaimed—more accurately than he knew—that he was a "God-thumpin', Bible-fearin' believer!"

Neo-orthodoxy

The most sophisticated interpretation of historic Christian faith on the conservative side of things in the last century was done by neo-orthodox theologians. Reacting against liberal nineteenth-century Protestantism, Karl Barth in Switzerland asked in 1918, What is the use of all the preaching, baptizing, confirming, bell-ringing, and organ playing, and so forth if *the critical event* (God addressing us in Christ) has not happened? He and others said that the **Christ of the creeds**, more than Jesus of history, needs to be re-presented. What especially inflamed neo-orthodox passion was, for them, a naive view about humanity. Two world wars (including the Holocaust) absolutely convinced new-orthodox thinkers that humanity was *not* progressing, *not* "getting better every day in every way." There was sin, and there was the need for a **savior** and for repentance.

There could not be "cheap grace," to quote Dietrich Bonhoeffer. He could speak on such subject because he knew the cost of discipleship; he was killed in a Nazi German prison because he participated in a plan to assassinate Adolf Hitler. With Barth and with Martin Niemoeller, Bonhoeffer proclaimed that only "Jesus is the Führer!" Another mostly neo-orthodox theologian, Paul Tillich, said Christians must keep "the Protestant principle" alive, the principle that says that God is *not* to be identified with a person (pope) or book (Bible) or system (capitalism) or anything that is penultimate. **Faith, only faith**, says he, will suffice. H. Richard Niebuhr at Yale Divinity School argued similarly, insisting that Christian faith at its best practices **radical monotheism**, which will have no other gods before God.

Neo-orthodoxy in the world of the twentieth century took several directions. It lent itself to various liberation theologies with value placed on **hope**. Such theology has ascended in third-world countries. Campesinos reading their Bible and reflecting on their world have come to believe in a God who has "a preferential option for the poor." African Americans adopted liberationist views of God in their struggle for civil rights. Women have struck for liberation too, insisting that the masculine casting of God be dropped for more inclusive images. Sallie McFague, for example, says we would be well served to think of God as **Mother, Lover, and Friend**, and she, furthermore, has spoken of "the earth as God's body." Thus she aligns herself with a creation spirituality emerging in the world today, which could be connected in Christian faith history with the Psalms, Duns Scotus Erigena, and Francis of Assisi.

McFague's move toward a more holistic picture of God is consistent with the best of Christian thinking over the millennia. Holistic thinking has also been a contribution of neo-orthodoxy, especially in terms of unity in the churches and with the world. Though the Church of Jesus Christ has splintered into churches—and continues to splinter—there is a thrust toward oneness of all things in God. The thrust echoes the biblical *Shema*: *Hear, O Israel, the Lord your God is* **one God**. The ecumenical movement of the last century has been at work bringing churches together and, more broadly, inviting Christians into dialogue with other-than-Christian brothers and sisters. Twenty-first-century men and women are in an ecumenical era—all in the same boat, Starship Earth, together. Faithful folk are being called back to the IDEA of **oneness in the Lord**.

Conclusion to Part 2

So . . . "God," over time, ever mediated.

In this part, much has been made over that which mediates God. Our best thinkers remind us that these mediations are *not* God. And yet we can never completely, nor for very long, divest ourselves of holy tokens, whether they are physical, mental, or emotional. They point to and remind us of God. Paul Tillich, in a discussion of symbols, says that "symbols participate in the reality" to which they point. So lovers of God have found many words, ways, and things to lead us to God, and—wonder of wonders—God sometimes comes back toward us in and through the symbols.

When we "draw nigh to God" in a church building, we know that our edifice has continuity with the temple in Jerusalem, a basilica in Constantinople, a cathedral in France, a meetinghouse in the Appalachians. When we pray, our prayers echo those of David, Augustine, and the Anglican *Book of Common Prayer*. When the liturgists intone, "Let us worship God," they stand with priests, prophets, and preachers of Shechem, Antioch, Wittenberg, and Cane Ridge. Creeds and faith statements that orient our thinking about God were shaped in the Sinai, Philippi, Nicaea, and Westminster. Music that now mediates the Holy has done so for congregations singing in monasteries, chapels, and storefront buildings. The Christ we look to has been prefigured in Moses, David, Elijah, and Cyrus, agonized over by Athanasius, Anselm, Calvin, and Kierkegaard, and praised as the revelation nonpareil. We proclaim God's oneness in company with Isaiah, Philo, Tertullian, Aquinas, Whitehead, and Niebuhr. We are ever before the Mystery approached by analogue and things visible and invisible.

Discussion Questions for Part 2: God

1. Think about your own evolving understanding of God. Over time, how has "God" changed? Have you moved from a simpler, concrete understanding of God to one more sophisticated and abstract? Have you gone the other way?

2. If God is always mediated, what are superior and inferior Christian mediations, so far as you and others in your community are concerned?

3. The author speculates on the origins of monotheism. Where would you come out on that discussion? How monotheistic is the current age?

4. Do you think the "God of the Older Testament" is different from the "God of the Newer Testament"? Why? Why not? How would these understandings differ from or be affirmed by the "God of the scientists"?

5. When all is said and done, the author seems to think that a Trinitarian way of talking about God is quite descriptive. Do you agree?

6. This part began with a quotation by Heinrich Zimmer: The best thing cannot be talked about; the second best will be misunderstood; and the third is not worth talking about. Why does the second create so much misunderstanding?

Part 3

Jesus

Jesus Christ is the same yesterday and today and tomorrow. Hebrews 13:8 (maybe, maybe not)

"Ecce homo!" exclaimed Pilate. John 19:5

"Who is that guy, anyway?" Butch Cassidy asked the Sundance Kid.

Someone once asked the question, "If Christ lived today, instead of 2000 years ago, how do you think he'd be regarded by the political establishment?"

"If Christ lived today . . . ?" The question baffles me. I thought he was living today. If not, could someone please tell me the meaning of the empty tomb? Maybe he went out to lunch? Or the meaning of the lives of all those who have died to say he lives, from the Apostles to, say, Archbishop Romero? Maybe they were all fools and charlatans? "How he would be regarded by the political establishment" is exactly how he is regarded by those who believe from the Apostles to Romero and follow through. He is in them capitally punished.

Daniel Berrigan, Priest

One of the most surprising things I ever saw was a stained-glass window of the Mount Stuart House in Rothesay, Scotland. There was a *Moses at the Burning Bush*. In the art piece, Moses had taken off his sandals and was standing awe-struck before the shrub ablaze yet not consumed. This was the occasion of Moses' great theophany (seeing the Holy). Yet in *this* depiction was something that seemed out of place. In the center of the burning bush were a Madonna and Child!

"How in the artist's imagination did they get there?" was my reaction.

Equal dissonance was created for me when viewing Lucas Cranach the Younger's *The Last Supper*, a 1565 CE painting. Around Jesus (who is clad in first-century attire) were sixteenth-century German burghers, including Martin Luther, Philipp Melanchthon, and the Prince of Anhalt, all in white frill collars!

Jesus has this wonderful way with his followers in which he is "read back" into older history and "thrown forward" in time, becoming contemporaneous with each age. Such back-and-forth presence is what this part of the book describes.

Originally I had planned *not* to do a part dedicated to Jesus, but, instead, simply to make him central in all the topical tracings. This was planned because, well . . . how do you put Jesus into the first two thousand years of our history when he hasn't even been born? On the other hand, how can we not focus on him? Clearly the tradition has always held that he is "prefigured" in the Older Testament. Moreover, Christian faith has always said we have a living Lord, one who has continued to be active over subsequent time with people, enlivening thought and devotion. He is not confined to the first third of the first century CE.

Jesus then has, at least, these three dimensions: (1) a pre-first-century formation, (2) a concrete historical time, and (3) a postresurrection life. We are talking about

- The power of God and humans that came to be embodied in him
- The power of his thirty-some earthly years, roughly 4 BCE to 30 CE
- The power of his spirit, memory, and influence moving through two millennia

If this is to be a basic *Christ*ianity book, we need to include our main man in his three dimensional powers.

So in this part of this book there is JESUS-1 as the Spirit, Word, and Wisdom of God to be "found" in the Older Testament that became incarnate in Jesus; in addition, fathers and mothers of the ancient faith came alive again in him; and there were things said of old that either seemed to point to him or were adopted by or for him. There is also in these pages JESUS-2, present in the flesh-and-blood man of Nazareth. His life, including resurrection from the tomb, we will consider. And then there is the postresurrection JESUS-3, who by the Holy Spirit has continued to develop in history, even into the Trinity, right to the present. He is the one we call our risen and living Lord, known in mystical union and concrete symbols.

For this discourse on Jesus, let me indicate to the reader initially where I am in my understanding and affection vis-à-vis Jesus. Later I will attempt a fuller personal appraisal.

Jesus the Christ is Lord for me, Emmanuel ("God with us"). I consider myself a Trinitarian Christian and a radical monotheist. Jesus is, existentially, "Savior," God incarnate, who (1) saves me from my worst self—my selfish, greedy, distracted, unfaithful, violent, prideful self, (2) sets me at peace with God, neighbor, and self, and (3) gives direction by calling me forward into a new order on earth as it is with God eternal. Jesus Christ is central in my life, even as I believe he is central to the history of our faith . . . and, ultimately, to the world.

(As we go through these chapters, I will capitalize major CHARACTERISTICS or CONCEPTS that are attributed to or emanate from Jesus and make bold the **names of people** who seem to prefigure him or become restatements of who he was and what he stood for.)

Chapter Seven

Jesus in Biblical Times

Premonarchic Millennium (2000–1000 BCE)

The Bible's opening words are "In the beginning God." The writer of the Gospel of John starts his story of Jesus, "In the beginning was the Word." The Word that John wants us to know is Jesus Christ (see John 1:17). Jesus as the Christ is for him the Son of God the Father, the one who was from the beginning, that is, at the time of creation, preexistent, there before all things were made. In theological language, the Word is *Logos*, and we should understand that, *in* Jesus, the LOGOS or WORD came to be embodied.

This is not to say that Jesus of Nazareth was "in the beginning," but that God as Word, which was there eternally, became incarnate (enfleshed) in time-bound Jesus. So Paul has it right when he says in 2 Corinthians 5:19 (KJV), "God was in Christ" and, if so, then we may hold that Christ was present at the start of all time and creation.

It is a bold claim, of course, but one central to Christian faith. The main point, for purposes of these chapters, is that (1) God created the world by the Word or Logos, which (2) was spoken by prophets and others, (3) became fully embodied in Jesus, and (4) continued to be heard and spoken by the people of God in Christ's church.

The above, then, is introduction to a major concept that came to be in Jesus. Jesus also is cast in roles of people thousands of years before his time. In the second chapter of Genesis we meet a Jesus-shaping person: **Adam**, the being "of earth." Theological tradition has it that Adam, the first man, fell from grace. In the popular version, he and "the woman" disobeyed instructions from God and, as a consequence, were expelled from the garden of Eden. Thus humankind became separated from God. What

81

the Newer Testament writers make of all this is that "in Christ" a **New Adam**, a new humanity, came into being. Paul especially works up the New Adam idea. So that, by the person and work of Jesus Christ, humanity is restored to right relationship with God. Paul says, "For since death came through a human being, the resurrection of the dead has also come through a human being; for as all die in Adam, so all will be made alive in Christ" (1 Cor. 15:21–22). What the Newer Testament interpreters of Jesus are doing is making explicit connections with the Older Testament, from God and Adam to Jesus.

It continues. The legendary ancestors, Abraham and Sarah, are of first-order significance, being the father and mother of faith. Two things in their story receive special consideration in understanding Jesus. The first is the account in Genesis 14, where a priest named **Melchizedek** of the ancient city of Salem (cf. Jeru-*salem*) came out and greeted Abram with bread and wine. Melchizedek is thought to have been in the priesting business long before there was an Aaronic or Levitic priesthood. He is mentioned in Psalm 110 as a priest of an everlasting order. In discussing the role of Jesus, the writer of the book of Hebrews says that Jesus is of the order of Melchizedek, "a priest forever," like no other priest before. Priest Jesus, he says, is able to make a perfect sinless sacrifice that all people may receive mercy and find grace.

To Abraham and Sarah was born a child whose name was **Isaac**. He was the one through whom a multitude of descendants were to come. That was the promise. But then came a command that this child was to be sacrificed. Obediently Abraham took Isaac—his only son Isaac—to Mount Moriah to kill him. We read:

> Isaac said to his father Abraham, "Father!"
> And he said, "Here I am, my son."
> He said, "The fire and the wood are here, but where is the lamb for a burnt offering?"
> Abraham said, "God himself will provide the lamb for a burnt offering."

Uh! As the Genesis 22 story goes, at the last minute Abraham was told to stop the murder and offer, instead, a ram caught in the thicket. In "The Binding of Isaac" (as this story is named in art), Christians hear what finally was done with Jesus: God provided God's self in the Lamb who is Jesus.

Two other Older Testament patriarchs deserve mention as "types" for the Jesus story. One is **Jacob** (the son of Isaac). Jacob had twelve sons—

the very number of disciples ascribed to Jesus, and you can be sure the number is significant. The other ancient typological figure is **Joseph**. He prefigured Jesus in many ways, but let me highlight two.

First, Joseph, though he was his father's favorite (receiving a long-sleeved coat or one of "many colors"), was rejected by his brothers and sold off to death in slavery. This REJECTION MOTIF is important to the early church's understanding of Jesus, as he too was spurned. Acts 7:9–10 retells Joseph's story on behalf of Jesus: "The patriarchs, jealous of Joseph, sold him into Egypt; but God was with him, and rescued him from all his afflictions." Newer Testament writers also lift up a line from Psalm 118:2 to let it be known that what happened to Jesus had precedent: "The stone that the builders rejected has become the cornerstone" (Matt. 21:42).

Second, Joseph was carried down to Egypt and eventually got all his family from Israel there. From Egypt these Israelites later escaped. When it comes to telling the Jesus story, the writer of the Gospel of Matthew has Jesus' holy family go down to Egypt (à la Joseph) and then come out (à la Moses).

Moses is simply huge in our faithparents' world. Having had to flee Egypt, Moses became a shepherd. In the great revelatory moment that Moses had before the burning bush, he asked God for God's name. Yahweh replied, "I AM WHO I AM." This self-designation of God was picked up by the writer of the Gospel of John. John says that Jesus issued seven "I AM" statements:

> I am the bread of life.
> I am the light of the world.
> I am the door of the sheep.
> I am the good shepherd.
> I am the resurrection and the life.
> I am the way, the truth, and the life.
> I am the true vine.

Even as Moses received the identifying name of God, so now Jesus added image-rich content regarding who he, as the Son of God, is and what he means for the world.

Jesus is the liberator and the lawgiver. He is very much cast in the image of Moses, especially in the Gospel of Matthew. When Jesus speaks, he delivers a Sermon on the Mount, and the reader will think of Mount Sinai, where Moses received the Ten Commandments. In Jesus' mountain sermon, he counsels faithfulness to the law and gives additional instruction:

"You have heard that it was said to those of ancient times, 'You shall not murder'; and 'whoever murders shall be liable to judgment.' But I say to you that if you are angry with a brother or sister, you will be liable to judgment" (Matt. 5:21–22). Matthew wants to convey that Moses was great . . . yet Jesus exceeds that greatness.

Finally, for this period, let us consider **Joshua.** Joshua, the Scriptures tell us, took over after Moses and led the former slaves into the promised land of Canaan. His name was the same as Jesus. Both mean, literally, "God saves." Joshua saved his people by winning the land for them; similarly Jesus, by victory over sin and death, saves people too long in the wilderness.

So, from this period of beginnings, we meet the ideas and people which/who are ever so important in our early history. We begin to see how they are woven into the life, works, and person of Jesus.

Time of the Kings and the Prophets (1000–550 BCE)

After the time of the judges (ca. 1200–1050 BCE) and a first attempt at kingship by Saul (just prior to 1000), we meet **David**, the shepherd boy and harpist who became Israel's greatest king. If you want to cast Jesus with anyone else of greatness in the Bible—besides Moses—it would be David. David is considered MESSIAH, one "anointed" by God, and so Jesus will come to be held. In eschatological thought ("end of time" thought) a messiah is expected to issue in a new kingdom of David. In the Newer Testament Jesus will often—about twenty times—be called "the son of David." David, among other things, united the tribes of Israel, defeated the Philistines, and made Jerusalem the center of their world. The early 1000s BCE is an apex in the memory of the Hebrew people, and certainly Jesus' followers saw him reembodying David.

To illustrate the identification of Jesus with David, there is the occasion when Jesus' followers plucked and ate corn on the Sabbath. Such behavior was a religious no-no. Jesus, though, reminded the critics of the similar action taken by David's men who on the Sabbath ate sacred bread from the very altar of God! The account suggests that scrupulous obedience to the law, which Jesus and his followers did *not* practice, was also *not* practiced by Israel's greatest king. So, the writer seems to say, don't get on Jesus' case unless you plan to censor David too.

Then, too, consider **Solomon** and the TEMPLE. Solomon was David's son, the king who maintained and expanded the empire and was the architect-builder of the temple of Jerusalem. This temple became the center of faith for the people of Israel. In it was the Holy of Holies, the room in which Yahweh was thought to dwell. Now came Jesus. He was closely associated with the temple (albeit, Herod's temple, the third since Solomon's). Jesus as an infant was taken to the temple for circumcision, and at twelve he was there again, this time conversing with the elders. As an adult he went to the temple as an observant worshipper and became distraught when he found the holy grounds desecrated by buyers and sellers. So he upended money changers' and merchants' tables. This is called the "cleansing of the temple," and was his symbolic way of proclaiming that a new kingdom was coming. The day after the cleansing, Jesus returned to the temple to teach and dispute with the chief priests and scribes. Finally, as his disciples left the city, they expressed awe about the temple; Jesus then replied enigmatically that the temple would be thrown down and then raised again in three days. He was, of course, referring to the resurrection and the temple of his body. What the Newer Testament writers are suggesting by all this attention to the temple is that the center of the faith—which had been in the Jerusalem temple—is now in Jesus, in his body, ultimately even in his body the church.

In addition, Solomon was credited with being a wise king. In time, a whole genre of literature and way of living called Wisdom was associated with him. We shall talk about WISDOM or Sophia in the next section of this chapter. Let it suffice to note here that Wisdom was connected to Solomon and would be seen as embodied in Jesus.

After the time of David and Solomon, the united kingdom broke apart into Israel and Judah. While the kings were important in these two realms and while there were priests in the temple(s), the religious power belonged to the prophets. Earliest among the prophets was **Elijah.**

Elijah spoke the WORD of the Lord, confronted a king and queen, contested with the prophets of Baal, restored a widow's son to life, had the mystical experience of hearing "a still small voice" on a mountaintop, and was carried into heaven on a fiery chariot. If this sounds like incidents from the life of John the Baptizer or Jesus, it should; both figures are cast à la Elijah. The still small voice experience is how the SPIRIT of God was given Elijah, and the Newer Testament says the Spirit was given to Jesus in a mountaintop experience too. When Jesus was transfigured on Mount Hermon, who then should appear with him but Moses and Elijah?! This showed that the Law (Moses) and the Prophets (Elijah) were with him, in him. The WORD or LOGOS and SPIRIT or *RUACH*, then, were embodied in Jesus.

In the Word and Spirit tradition also stood the eighth-century BCE prophets. Jesus would wear their mantle. One prophet was **Amos,** from the little town of Tekoa in the south. He went north to the religious center of Shechem. There he spoke out for the needy, widows, and orphans and against the powerful and wealthy who ground down the poor. His passion was for the justice and righteousness of God, and he spoke of a day of the Lord (Amos 5:18). Jesus stood in this speaking-out WORD tradition of Amos, calling for repentance and the Basileia of God. Other prophets—**Hosea, Isaiah of Jerusalem**, and **Jeremiah**—were speakers of such a Word too.

Jesus also was recipient of understandings by **Second Isaiah**, prophet of the mid-sixth century BCE, who had witnessed the fall of Jerusalem to the Babylonians in 586. (The destruction of the northern kingdom by the Assyrians had occurred in 722 BCE.) As Second Isaiah wrote, he saw the SUFFERING of the people who were forced into foreign captivity. He knew about their suffering, their being despised, shamed, abhorred, and rejected. Since he believed that God was going to enable the exiles to return home, he found meaning in their pain. Telling of that suffering, as if Israel the people were *one* person, Isaiah wrote,

> Surely he has borne our infirmities and carried our diseases. . . . But he was wounded for our transgressions, crushed for our iniquities; upon him was the punishment that made us whole, and by his bruises we are healed. . . . He was oppressed, and he was afflicted, yet he did not open his mouth. . . . By a perversion of justice he was taken away . . . cut off from the land of the living. . . . They made his grave . . . with the rich, although he had done no violence, and there was no deceit in his mouth. . . . [H]e bore the sin of many, and made intercession for the transgressors. (Isa. 53:4–12)

As noted above, Second Isaiah probably was referring to the people Israel rather than any individual (before or later), but Jesus himself may have heard and understood these words and in some sense consciously enacted them during his own trial, passion, and passing. Certainly later Christians saw in such "**servant** passages" (Isaiah 42, 49, 50, and 52–53) much of what happened to Jesus and even what it meant in terms of suffering and redemption for themselves—and all people.

And then there is **Third Isaiah**, to whom chapters 56–66 of the book of Isaiah are attributed. In Isaiah 61:1–2, in the best prophetic tradition, he says,

> The spirit of the Lord GOD is upon me, because the LORD has anointed me; he has sent me to bring good news to the oppressed, to

bind up the brokenhearted, to proclaim liberty to the captives, and release to the prisoners; to proclaim the year of the LORD's favor.

The idea of the SPIRIT of God figures prominently in Newer Testament understandings of Jesus. In fact the passage above is reported to have been read by him in the synagogue of Nazareth as he began his ministry. "The Spirit of the Lord is upon me . . ." (Luke 4:18), Jesus read, and then he added, "Today this scripture has been fulfilled in your hearing" (Luke 4:21). Above all else, Jesus was a "Spirit-Person." The Gospel writers say that Spirit came to Jesus at his birth, his baptism, and on the mount of transfiguration.

Second Temple Period (550–20 BCE)

Second Isaiah's words of release from suffering and captivity in Babylon came true in 538 BCE. In that year **Cyrus the Persian**, conqueror of the Babylonians, allowed exiled people to return to their homes. For the Judean exiles, Cyrus was a gift from God. They understood him as MESSIAH, one "anointed" by God, to fulfill a winning and redeeming role on behalf of God's people. In time Jesus would be designated and understood by his postresurrection followers as a messiah—even *the* messiah of God. When the term is translated into Greek, it becomes **"Christ."** Within a decade or so after Jesus' death and resurrection, it is essentially his name: Jesus the Christ, or Jesus the Anointed, or Jesus the Messiah.

In the late sixth century BCE, when the exiles returned to Jerusalem, they did three things: they rebuilt the temple, put up a wall around Jerusalem so that the city was defensible, and collected the books ("Bible," literally) that for them became sacred Scripture. The last meant that our foreparents in the faith assembled the sundry writings from the previous five hundred years and turned them into what would be called the Law and the Prophets.

Among the prophets were Ezekiel and Daniel. In describing their vision for the future of the people, they used a special term for one who is in relation to God: **son of man**. Ninety-three times Ezekiel speaks of himself as a "son of man," meaning "human being." Jesus describes himself by the moniker too. In Daniel the name is used to describe an apocalyptic figure. He wrote an enormously influential text:

As I watched in the night visions, I saw one like a human being, coming with the clouds of heaven. And he came to the Ancient One [i.e.,

God] and was presented before him. To him was given dominion and glory and kingship, that all peoples, nations, and languages should serve him. (Dan. 7:13–14)

So the name "son of man" is loaded with meanings both human and divine, especially as it later came to be *the* designation that Jesus used in speaking of himself. He is the Son of Man, the human one, closely connected to God in a coming judgment.

Ezekiel and Daniel were written late in the Second Temple period, about the time as the extrabiblical books of Esdras and Enoch, which also use the title "son of man." All these books were written after the Persians had been ousted from power by the Greeks (under Alexander the Great, who is *not* designated a messiah). The Greeks come to exercise huge influence on the Hebrew people and eventually provoked them into an uprising in the middle of the second century BCE. The revolt, amazingly enough, was successful! The brothers Maccabees, who led the anti-Greek forces, were seen as sons of men who began to wear a title of "anointed" as well. People in Jesus' time may well have been looking for a messiah who would act more like an anointed king and lead a revolt against the Romans.

(It was the Romans who controlled Palestine before, during, and after Jesus' day. In 63 BCE Pompey had taken over in Palestine, and in 40 BCE the Roman emperor made Herod king. In 20 BCE he rebuilt the Jerusalem temple to a glory it had not had for half a millennium.)

Finally, for this period, let us note developments more philosophical. As Jews of the Diaspora spread out in the Gentile world, they became acquainted with Greek thought. Greek thought about God was more abstract and speculative than Hebrew. The Greeks loved SOPHIA or WISDOM, and they thought people should be guided by Wisdom's ways into what is right and wrong. Jewish thinkers came to agree with the idea and tried to make it fit with their older religious sensibilities. So Wisdom literature was written by Jews, as reflected in Proverbs, Job, Ecclesiastes, some psalms, and several extracanonical books. Wisdom was a high ideal, clearly related to God, that is, of God. It was seen as "the way in which to go, to walk." Even the law was conceived of as Lady Wisdom herself.

In Newer Testament times, then, Jesus was perceived as the embodiment of Wisdom. He knew how to walk in the way of God, how to choose the good and avoid evil. Paul spoke of Jesus as "the power of God and the wisdom of God" (1 Cor. 1:24). Theologian Elizabeth Johnson says,

What Judaism said of Sophia, Christian hymn makers and epistle writers now came to say of Jesus: he is image of the invisible God (Col. 1:15); the radiant light of God's glory (Heb. 1:3); the one through whom all things were made (I Cor. 8:6). . . . As the trajectory of wisdom Christology shows, Jesus was so closely associated with Sophia that by the end of the first century he is presented not only as a wisdom teacher, not only as a child and envoy of Sophia, but ultimately as an embodiment of Sophia herself.[1]

Greek influence on Hebrew thought guided what was later concluded about Jesus. Greek peripatetic ways, as practiced by Cynic philosophers, may also have influenced how Jesus lived out his ministry—as an itinerate rabbi and wisdom teacher.

As we conclude this section, let me repeat what was said earlier: the Older Testament does not "foretell" the coming of Jesus but (1) certain biblical features related to God became alive in Jesus, in particular, notions about WORD, SPIRIT, and WISDOM, and (2) certain biblical figures also seem to characterize him, in particular, **Moses, David, the suffering servant, and the son of man.** I call this a Jesus-1 presentation, to indicate the preparation power for the historical Jesus, whom I call Jesus-2.

Now let us lift up Jesus-2, a man of the Middle East in the first century of the Common Era (CE)—called AD, *anno Domini*, "in the year of the Lord," in earlier histories.

Newer Testament Times (20 BCE-110 CE)

To this point, we have been discussing Jesus in terms of ATTRIBUTES and **persons** that helped early Christians interpret their experience of Jesus. Now we turn to his life story as lived in history. It is told best in the Gospels, though not really as biography—CNN was not there—but as "good news" accounts, that readers might believe in him. The roughly parallel chronologies found in the *Synoptic* ("seeing the same way") Gospels of Matthew, Mark, and Luke constitute a compatible life of Jesus. Many churches today also follow his "life" according to the Synoptic Gospels in their Christian calendar year, Advent through Pentecost, especially. As part of a worship service cycle, there are hymns that tell much of Jesus' life, death, and resurrection. Instead of recounting Jesus' story in prose narrative, let us look at mostly familiar church hymnody. Consider this as Jesus' story from the Gospels:

A Life of Jesus in Songs

Birth

Word of God, Come Down on Earth (incarnation)
Come, O Long-Expected Jesus
Mary, Woman of the Promise (mother)
Gentle Joseph, Joseph Dear (father)
O Little Town of Bethlehem (birthplace)
Away in a Manger
Silent Night, Holy Night
While Shepherds Watched Their Flocks by Night
Angels, from the Realms of Glory
We Three Kings
Jesus, Jesus, Oh, What a Wonderful Child

Life and Ministry

The Baptist Shouts on Jordan's Shore
Lord Jesus, Who through Forty Days (temptation)
Jesus Calls Us, o'er the Tumult (gathering disciples)
When Jesus the Healer Passed through Galilee (healings)
"Silence! Frenzied, Unclean Spirit" (exorcism)
Break Now the Bread of Life (miracles)
Blessed Are the Poor in Spirit (preaching)
The Kingdom of God (teachings)
Jesus Is the Friend of Sinners
Christ, upon the Mountain Peak (transfiguration)
A Woman Came Who Did Not Count the Cost (anointing)
Jesus Met the Woman at the Well
Jesus Loves Me! (blessing children)
"I Am the Light of the World"

Crucifixion

Jesus Walked This Lonesome Valley (face to Jerusalem)
Ride On! Ride On in Majesty (triumphal entry)
[No song known regarding cleansing the temple]
Christ at Table, There with Friends (Last Supper)
Go to Dark Gethsemane (final night)
He Never Said a Mumblin' Word (trial)

Were You There When They Crucified My Lord?
O Sacred Head, Now Wounded
Alas! and Did My Savior Bleed

Resurrection

I Come to the Garden Alone
Christ the Lord Is Risen Today
The Day of Resurrection
He Lives
Abide with Me (Road to Emmaus)

Postresurrection

Christ Enthroned in Heavenly Splendor (ascension)
On Pentecost They Gathered (Spirit)
Spirit of the Living God (Parousia)
Christ Will Come Again

General

Lord of the Dance
Amen, Amen (life of Jesus)

More than songs *about* Jesus are hymns of praise and exaltation *to* and *for* Jesus. Here are a few: *All Hail the Power of Jesus' Name; Blessed Assurance, Jesus Is Mine; Jesus, the Very Thought of You; Jesus, Lover of My Soul; What a Friend We Have in Jesus; I Love to Tell the Story; Fairest Lord Jesus; Crown Him with Many Crowns;* and *O for a Thousand Tongues to Sing.* There are ever so many more.

The "central event" of the Christian story (see this book's part 1) is the resurrection of Jesus Christ. He is the "main character" in our faith drama. What we believe about "God" (concern of part 2 of this book) is very much derived from Jesus. These are some of the things said already. In the next few pages we are dealing directly with his advent, character, works, and person.

As a pastor, when I teach a new members' class, I often ask what about Jesus is most important. Here are some typical answers:

that he was born (Christmas being so big)
what he did—healings and miracles
his teachings, "definitely his teaching"
who he was
that he died "for my sins"

that he rose from the dead
that he intercedes for us in heaven

In my estimation, the answer is "that he rose from the dead." THE RES-URRECTION is the sine qua non about Jesus. His overcoming death—however that occurred, physically or symbolically or both—has made all the difference.

After that? Jesus' crucifixion. His death was so important that the first writer of material for the Newer Testament, Paul, spent considerable time thinking through its meaning and significance.

Christ's resurrection, first, and his crucifixion, second, prompted people to want to know, third, who he was, what he taught and did, who his friends were, how he prayed, where he came from.

After that, perhaps, they were interested to find out who his parents were, where he was born, and so on. So those were written down, fourth. His history, then, is written backward from Easter.

The God-Man and his story had a double effect. For one thing, it sent followers scurrying back to locate him in the Older Testament, to find "evidence of foretelling," like Jesus precast in the role of suffering servant à la Isaiah; some scurrying sent Word-Spirit-Wisdom into his story. Similarly, Jesus' story sent folks running forward, trying to appropriate his life for their lives and figure out who he was as the postresurrection Jesus.

In this latter concern, the focus was on trying to save the MEANING of Jesus to individuals, the community of faith, and the world. New Testament scholars Marcus Borg and Paula Fredrikson in their talks and writings sometimes give summary historical sketches on Jesus.[2] They could be quoted, but, the reader indulging me, let me say what I have concluded about Jesus, after having followed him for a lifetime.

I have no doubt that there was a Jesus of Nazareth, a real-life, flesh-and-blood human being who walked the hills of Palestine during the first third of the first century of the Common Era. He was, first of all, a teacher-prophet, a gifted communicator, interesting, gutsy, and one passionately committed to God. He attracted devoted disciples (female and male) who liked his message and way of life. His message was about a Basileia or reign of God that was breaking into the world—and soon. This Basileia of God ("domination-free order") had a quality of relationship in which there was plenteous forgiveness, love of God and neighbor, justice, and hope. Because of his commitments, Jesus came into conflict with significant authorities—religious and political—which caused him to be sent to the cross. But he made the crucifixion a supreme example of self-giving love. He died on the cross, was buried . . . and God raised him from death. This was God's great Yes to the man and to the world. (Now we get to the MEANING dimension.) I believe that Jesus Christ is, therefore, **the window into God and the mirror of true humanity.** *Though there may be other religious ways unto God in the world, I do not need to look for another. Jesus the Christ let loose in the world a virus of reconciliation that is still at work and will, in God's time, ultimately prevail. His revelation of God's way—or, God's revelation through him—into love and forgiveness makes him* **the Savior of the world.**

We might say much more about Jesus, that he was a charismatic personality, brilliant storyteller, faith healer, miracle worker, exorcist, host for open table fellowship. And more. There will always be more to say. Certainly he developed what nineteenth-century theologian Friedrich Schleiermacher called "God-consciousness." He was a spirit person, a person of God, who thought deeply and prayed constantly and worked to align himself with the will of God. He became a child of God, as we all may be, but he became so much so that he has come to be, for people from two thousand years ago to the present, *the* Son of God.

It is fair to ask, "Did Jesus think of himself as God?"

The answer I would give is No. He spoke of himself only as "Son of man" or "the human one"—some eighty-two times in the Gospels. Asked once about his goodness, Jesus replied, "Why do you call me good? No one is good but God alone" (Mark 10:18). I do not believe that Jesus believed he was born of a virgin, could call down angels to help him, had power to walk on water, could calm storms, multiply loaves and fishes, or do many other things that are attributed to him. These sorts of things are more nearly "explanations of the experience" of Jesus, as Bishop John Shelby Spong suggests.[3] I believe that he was "like us in every way" and "knew exactly the life we know" with all its joy and frustrations, successes and failures, toothaches, and temptations. Considering the prominence in the gospels of Mary Magdalene, I am open to the possibility, highlighted by the runaway bestseller *The Da Vinci Code* by Dan Brown, that he was not celibate. Perhaps Jesus was married to Mary Magdalene. Jesus was a man.

It is his very humanity, his full humanity, that makes him savior to individuals and to the world. As the church father Gregory of Nazianzus said, "What God could not assume, God could not save." So what God did in Jesus is assume full humanity, that **Jesus** might become CHRIST.

At what moment was God "in Christ"? Well, as John tells it, from the beginning of time. Luke and Matthew suggest that the fullness of divinity came to dwell in Jesus at the time of conception by the Holy Spirit. The writer of the Gospel of Mark suggests that the moment of incarnation occurred at his baptism; then the Spirit came down saying, "You are my beloved Son." A case could be made for deification, if you will, happening at Mount Hermon, at the time of his mystical transfiguration. Any one of these is fine, but I am taken by an idea that I think I first heard from theologian Paul Tillich, that it was only on the cross that the fullness of divinity came. It is as if Jesus had to live out his full humanity and then, in surrender and trust, offer himself to God. At that moment the fullness of God entered Jesus. This is, to be sure, "adoptionist" heresy condemned by church councils, but I like the idea that, on the cross, humanity is stretched up toward God, so that divinity might stretch down to the human being!

The Christology offered above is a reverse take on the *kenosis* or "emptying" theology found in Paul's letter to the church in Philippi, chapter 2, verses 5–11:

> Let the same mind be in you that was in Christ Jesus, who, though he was in the form of God, did not count equality with God as something to be exploited, but emptied himself, taking the form of a slave, being born in human likeness. And being found in human form, he humbled himself and became obedient to the point of death—even death on a cross. Therefore God also highly exalted him and gave him the name that is above every name, so that at the name of Jesus, every knee should bend . . . and every tongue should confess that **Jesus Christ is Lord,** to the glory of God the Father.

I do not think Jesus knew that he was the Lord or "the revelation of God." If somehow he knew, he divested himself, emptied himself (*kenosis*), of that knowledge that he might be fully human. *Then* the fullness of God might come again to him. That, I conjecture, happened on the cross.

Jesus died.

Now the surprise: God raised him! Jesus' most devoted female friend, Mary Magdalene, and possibly some other women, went to his tomb to anoint his body with burial spices. When they got there, they found the stone sealing the burial cave rolled back and the tomb's corpse-ledge empty. He was not there. The chains of death had been broken. Jesus was back in life again, "back in play," appearing to Mary, Peter, John, disciples in an upper room, two followers on the road to Emmaus, by the seaside in Galilee, as well as on a mountain there. The resurrection appearances in the Newer Testament Gospels come as fireworks bursting in the air, and there is little point in trying to "make sense" of it all, except to say, "Something happened!" And that has made all the difference. In Jesus' resurrection an affirmation of life was spoken in the face of all the world's negativities.

(A psychological explanation—which may be the only kind modern people can hear—might suggest that the crestfallen followers of Jesus went back to Galilee to resume their previous lives. When they gathered, though, they might have begun to say, "What he said is still true. What he stood for (the Basileia of God) is still right. What he said about God is still valid. Everything about him is worth remembering, living by, and telling others of." And, in so recognizing the ongoing worth of all Jesus said/did/was, it was as if he were alive. He was resurrected in their mind and life. To explain that, they generated the "walk to Emmaus" story (Luke 24) that, for moderns, may be the best of the half-dozen postresurrection "appearance" accounts.)

Whatever happened and however it happened, the followers of Jesus came to speak of him in postresurrection ways. He became the postresurrection JESUS, whom I call Jesus-3, understood as alive and active in the world, sometimes as the Holy Spirit and sometimes as the risen Lord . . . but of the same piece, which is God.

As noted above, the earliest writings we have about Jesus were done by Paul. He uses the phrase "in Christ God was reconciling the world to himself" (2 Cor. 5:19a). Stephen Neill, Bible scholar and mission historian, has a book called *Jesus through Many Eyes*. In it he shows how the several authors of the Newer Testament have different "takes" on Jesus, some of which we have discussed already. Mark, the earliest Gospel writer, pictures Jesus as more of a **messianic prophet**. Matthew shows him as the **law-giver**, à la Moses. Luke has a gentler, **inclusive Jesus**. And John presents Jesus as the **self-conscious Son of God**, giving signs and making "I AM" statements. Each of the writers of the epistles has a unique interpretation of Jesus too. In James he is a **doer**, in Hebrews **high priest** of the order of Melchizedek, and so on.

Neill believes that in all the writings there is agreement that Jesus is primarily about (1) resurrection, (2) Spirit, and (3) reconciliation.[4] The post-Easter followers of Jesus are in consensus that to look at Jesus is, somehow, to see the face of God . . . *and* the face of our humanity as God intended it to be. All these "sightings" have not exhausted the meaning possibilities. One has to love what John says about Jesus near the end of his Gospel:

> Now Jesus did many other signs in the presence of his disciples, which are not written in this book. But these are written so that you

may come to believe that Jesus is the Messiah, the Son of God, and that through believing you may have life in his name. (John 20:30–31)

[T]here are also many other things that Jesus did; if every one of them were written down, I suppose that the world itself could not contain the books that would be written. (John 21:25)

Chapter Eight

Jesus in the Early Church

Struggling Centuries of the Church (110–500 CE)

The earliest Christians believed they had to be in mission. The mission turned out to be both geographical and intellectual. Their risen Lord had told them to "go into all the world," and they went, creating a Christian presence around the Mediterranean in less than a hundred years. The Jesus Christ they proclaimed in missionary sermons is told of in the kerygma (core message) that the apostles preached; here is one by Peter:

> We must obey God rather than any human authority. The God of our ancestors *raised up Jesus*, whom you had killed by hanging him on a tree. God exalted him at his right hand as Leader and Savior that he might give repentance to Israel and forgiveness of sins. And we are witnesses to these things, and so is the Holy Spirit whom God has given to those who obey him. (Acts 5:29–32, emphasis added)

Certainly it is this **risen Christ** who was proclaimed to the world in the decades after his resurrection. And Christ's SPIRIT was also found to be present, as told by the apostle Paul, who was blinded on the road to Damascus and confronted by the voice of Christ. The Christ who was brought out in the kerygmatic sermons is one who offered hope in a troubled, imperial Roman world.

The "good news" the apostle preached was not necessarily good news to all hearers. Though Jesus and his immediate followers were Jews, not all Jews were receptive. It was not so much the idea of Jesus as the **Son of God** that troubled traditional synagogue believers as it was that Jesus and his followers were not observant enough about the law and its requirements of circumcision and kosher food. That—and the dangerous talk of Jesus' imminent return, issuing in a "new kingdom"—were perceived as dangerous by Jews in the Diaspora. They feared that talk of a new Basileia (or reign) might bring down Roman wrath. Whatever the reason, there was rejection of Christ.

Kerygma presentations such as Peter's, though, were received as good or better news by Gentile God-fearers, who had been earlier attracted to the faith of Abraham and Moses. These Gentiles liked what they heard about Jesus, his way of life, his Basileia of God, and his coming again through the Holy Spirit.

Gentiles, of course, were familiar with other religious worldviews and philosophies, especially Greek, which were prevalent at the time. They insisted that a religion be philosophically grounded. They would not submit to just any idea. What Christian "apologists" (explainers) had to do was figure out how to make Jesus make sense to intrigued Gentiles. The apologists used two Greek concepts, *ousia* and *hypostasis*, to talk about God. They said that while God's *ousia* (essence or substance) is unknowable (as Greek philosophy held), God's *hypostases* (powers or accidents or characteristics) could be viewed from without. This line of thinking led the second-century CE Christian apologist Tertullian to talk about THE TRINITY. He spoke of "one God in three Persons," where "persons" meant masks, *hypostases*, accidents, or manifestations. The three persons in the Trinity were Father, Son, and Holy Spirit. Jesus was the **Son** or **second member of the Trinity**, in whom the fullness (essence) of divinity dwelt.

Even as the early church thinkers were working hard to explain their faith to the wider world, the Romans came down on this errant branch of Judaism. At various times and places, the people of the Way were persecuted. Not a few saw the face of Jesus as they endured death on crosses or were torn apart by wild animals in coliseums.

The story of Polycarp, the Bishop of Smyrna about 150 years after Jesus, is wonderfully illustrative. During the time of a Roman persecution he was sought by the authorities but spirited away by friends to a little farm in the country. The soldiers found him, though, and, in taking him back to town, the high sheriff, whose wife was a Christian asked, "What is the harm in saying, 'Caesar is Lord' and putting some incense on the altar, thus saving yourself?"

Polycarp said he could not and, so, was brought into the arena to be thrown to lions. The governor gave him three chances to save his life.

First, he ordered Polycarp to say, "Away with the atheists" (that is, away with Christians who did not believe in the Roman gods).

What Polycarp did, instead, was point to the crowd in the galleries and say, "Away with the atheists!"

The governor gave him another chance, "Curse Christ."

Polycarp answered, "Eighty and six years have I served him and he has done me no wrong, and can I revile my King that saved me?"

A third time the governor asked, "Swear by Christ." Polycarp answered, "I am a Christian. If you want to know what that is, set a day and listen."

"I'll throw you to the beasts," the governor threatened.

"Bring on your beasts," said Polycarp.

"If you scorn beasts, I'll have you burned."

"Better the fire that burns for an hour than the fire of hell that never goes out."

So Polycarp was burned at the stake. Here is his dying prayer, "Lord God Almighty, Father of Jesus Christ, I bless thee that thou didst deem me worthy of this hour. . . . May I be an acceptable sacrifice. I praise thee, I bless thee, I glorify thee through Jesus Christ."

Martyrdoms, mercifully, came to an end in 313 when new Roman emperors issued an edict of toleration, ending persecution. Then in 325, Constantine, now the sole emperor, called Christian bishops together in Nicaea, near his soon-to-be capital, Constantinople. At Nicaea the clerics hammered out the classic Nicene Creed, which officially formulated the doctrine of the Trinity. Council bishops agreed that the Son was "of one substance (*ousia*, essence) with the Father."

Having fixed Christ's position in relationship to the Father and to the Spirit, there then arose in Christian intellectual circles questions of how he could be both God and man. Was he half god, half man? God only, but in the appearance of a man? Human in body, divine in mind? What? And *when* was he the Son of God? From the beginning? Or was he the creation of the Father? These were not unsubstantial questions, and it took the church centuries to figure out doctrinal formulae that were acceptable to the majority. Finally, at the Council of Chalcedon in 451 CE, church leaders agreed that Jesus Christ is one person in "Two Natures": **Divine**, being of the same substance with the Father, and **Human**, being of the same substance as all people. These two natures, they said, were united unconfusedly, unchangeably, indivisibly, and inseparably in him.

To people of the twenty-first century these definitions may seem like much ado about little, but they were hugely important then. They are not inconsequential now. In keeping with Nicaea and Chalcedon, we might keep in mind that the name "Jesus Christ" says it well, as it speaks of humanity ("Jesus") and divinity ("Christ"). The image I find most helpful is one given above, that of Jesus as WINDOW and MIRROR. If someone wants to know what God is like or who she or he is called to be, look to Jesus, the **God-man**, the one fully divine and fully human.

Through these early centuries there was much defining, arguing, even warfare over questions of orthodoxy (right belief). In the West a growing consensus came in the early fifth century with Augustine's relational understanding of the Trinity. Some call it a psychological theory. Augustine suggested that, just as in one person there is "being, knowing and willing," so there is the same in the Godhead. Or, to use other words, God's internal life has unity established by existing, thinking, and loving, attributes that mutually and completely interpenetrate. Christ offers, according to Augustine, more of the THINKING aspect, whereas loving is more from the Spirit, who holds Father and Son together. The "work" that Augustine held Christ did was winning the eternal salvation of humanity, overcoming our fallen state that began with Adam and Eve. Christ became the means of God's GRACE, "grace" being of utmost significance to Augustine—as with Paul before him. Salvation, Augustine said, was not won by human achievement but by God's love alone, offered freely in Christ Jesus. Our appropriate response is faith in God through Christ.

The Age of Monasticism (500-1100 CE)

In the second half of the first millennium CE, Jesus' face became leaner and sterner, the face of an **ascetic** and a **judge**. The leaner image was brought on by the growing importance in the church of monks and nuns. When persecution of Christians stopped in the fourth century, many Christians decided that, in order to live faithfully, they needed to model their lives on the SUFFERING Christ. They took seriously his words in Mark 8:34: "If any want to become my followers, let them deny themselves and take up their cross and follow me." So men took to the desert to be solitary monks (hermits), such as the sainted **Antony**. Others joined in drawn-apart communities to live by a rule for community life, as laid down by Pachomius, for example. Women as well as men joined this movement of separation from the world, becoming nuns in convents. The Jesus who seemed to dominate their thinking was the ascetic Jesus, who spent forty days in the wilderness praying and fasting, overcoming temptations. This Jesus denied his body to live in the spirit with God, and, of course, he suffered and was eventually crucified.

As Jesus' followers, monks and nuns tried to live lives of self-denial. They took vows of celibacy, as they believed Christ lived. They practiced poverty, taking seriously Jesus' words to give away possessions and to come follow him. They were obedient to their superiors as to Christ. *Ora et labora* ("pray and work"), the main guidelines for conduct laid down by Benedict's Rule of 540, were the order of every day. Jesus of the monks and nuns was not the one who attended weddings and banquets, came playing a flute and dancing, and was accused of being a winebibber. He was more akin to John the Baptizer: serious, wearing rough clothes, wailing and weeping, eating no bread and drinking no wine. A leaner Jesus, then, was the one presented in the world through the monks and nuns.

Jesus was also sterner, more of a judge. During the first centuries of the church, Jesus was most often depicted as a young shepherd with a lamb on his shoulders. At the beginning of the Middle Ages, he became an older, distant, severe potentate. He seemed to merge with God the Father (as the Son was in the Godhead) to become what Orthodox Christians call the Pantocrator, Christ the all sovereign, the Judge of all the earth, the cosmic Christ. Icons of Christ Pantocrator were painted or made of mosaics on the dome ceilings of sanctuaries, so the powerful Holy One was looking down on his people. With one hand Christ Pantocrator blessed them (literally, with his thumb-to-ring-finger sign), while in the other hand he held the book of Names, record of who is in and who is out of heaven. In the Pantocrator, Christ was certainly lifted up "to judge the quick and the dead." It was a generally fearsome Lord, aloof, eyes dark and penetrating, no smile on his lips.

(Partly because of Christ's imaged sternness, Mary the mother of Jesus—also called the Theotokos [God-Bearer]—more and more came to be venerated and called upon as a mediator between the faithful and God.)

The Jesus we meet during these centuries, then, is ascetic and austere.

As devoted as were the monks in their cloisters and priests in their basilicas (churches) to such a Jesus and given to praising him, they were also responsible during this period for much of the expansion of Christianity. After the Germanic tribes overran western Europe and effectively shrank Christianity, disciplined monks from Ireland started east replanting the faith. Pope Gregory the Great in Rome in the late 500s sent the monk Augustine (of Canterbury) to England to reestablish the church there. In the East, the monks Cyril and Methodius went toward Slavic people in the north, introducing Eastern Orthodox Christianity, and in 988 Christianity came to Russia. Dedicated, self-denying, Jesus-loving monks made the spread possible. Expansion to the north kept Orthodoxy strong while many former locales of strength (Antioch, Jerusalem, Alexandria) were, from the seventh century CE, increasingly under Islamic dominance.

On the theological front in this era, one of the concerns that dominated thought in the Western church (but little in the East) was what Christ's death on the cross *meant*. What "work" had he done in giving his life? Two major interpretations occurred in this time, both of which are with us yet. One came from Anselm of Canterbury in his important book *Cur Deus Homo* (Why the God-Man?). He developed a theory of the ATONE-MENT (at-one-ment, making peace between God and humans), saying that Christ died to satisfy the offended honor of God, which was violated by people's sin. Jesus, the sinless one, offered his life; this satisfied the just demands of God and thus won our salvation. Jesus could do this, of course, because God was with him.

Anselm's view of the necessary work of Christ has been dominant in thinking through later centuries. It should be noted, though, that other understandings of the meaning of the cross are available. Most notably, Peter Abelard (who overlaps Anselm in the eleventh century) had a different take. He said Christ reconciles us to God by the EXAMPLE OF LOVE. Christ, he believed, modeled the way of forgiveness and love right to and through his death. We are reconciled to God—made at one—as we live in his *agape* (loving) way, Abelard said. This is the exemplarist theory of the atonement, which has enjoyed better reception in recent decades.

High Christendom Years (1100–1450 CE)

Abelard's exemplar Christ became embodied during the early centuries of the second millennium in **Francis of Assisi** and his Order of Friars Minor. Francis decided to follow the monastic way of poverty, chastity, and obedience but to do it differently, not set apart in the desert or chanting in a monastery, but by serving *in the world*. He instituted a mendicant or begging order, following Jesus' instructions to go out carrying no provisions, receiving what people will offer, and proclaiming God's love in selfless service. The going out, however, was done in joy and freedom. He said of his poverty, "I have married a beautiful lady, Madame Poverty!" Francis's work drew thousands to it in very few years.

Accompanying the Franciscans along their way were two other new orders of brothers, the Dominicans and the Norbertines. The Dominicans went out to preach for conversion or return of the wayward to the faith. White-robed Norbertines also preached and led in church reform.

With the Franciscans, the Dominicans, and the Norbertines we see a kinder, gentler Jesus, servant of the people, proclaimer of peace. Jaroslav Pelikan in *Jesus through the Centuries* notes that many consider Francis to be the **Second Christ**.[1] His way of living out Jesus was articulated by a fifteenth-century follower, Thomas à Kempis, who wrote one of the most widely read books of all time, *Imitation of Christ*.

The lowly way of Christ, however, was not the only way. In fact, we also see quite the opposite during the late Middle Ages. Christus Victor, the conquering Christ, came to be, especially after Pope Urban II in 1095 CE called for a holy war to reclaim the "Holy Lands" from the Muslims. Those who responded to his summons went out as "crusaders," on the basis of the *crux* (cross) they carried into battle or wore on their uniforms. So Jesus of Nazareth, Prince of Peace, became the militant Christ leading into holy war.

Two hundred years of war in the Middle East won nothing for the princes and prelates of the Christian West. Moreover, they weakened the Orthodox Church and the Christian Byzantine Empire. Besides unifying the Arabs, the crusaders captured and sacked the Christian City of Constantinople. A weakened Constantinople thus fell to Ottoman Turks in 1453. In time it took its current name, Istanbul.

One might hold that all this war and destruction in Christ's name would only serve to sadden our Lord, in essence, to *crucify* him again. Perhaps this is the reason that the **crucified Christ** rose to such "popularity" during these centuries. Statuary with a tormented Jesus nailed to a cross began to dominate in the Roman Church. Moreover, Western churches established within their walls "stations of the cross" in remembrance of Jesus' passion. He became the bleeding, dying savior—perhaps a reflection of ordinary people's own agony in a brutal feudal system.

Alternatives to the predominantly crucified Jesus took three forms. First, he became **the Christ child** in Madonna and child paintings, as the faithful sensed the need for a more feminine side to their savior. Second, Jesus became more of a **mystic**, as mysticism came into its own in northern Europe and England; a book, *The Cloud of Unknowing*, recalled the transfigured Jesus on Mount Hermon with Moses and Elijah in a cloud. Male and female contemplatives prayed *through* Jesus Christ who had said he was "one with the Father." A third Christ came into reality during this time: the **universal Christ**. The Renaissance flowered in Italy, made possible because of exposure to Islamic and Byzantine cultures. The science, art, and culture of ancient Greece, including the lost works of Aristotle, entered the West. A burst of creative energy and learning went on; trade expanded; a better money economy emerged. With new optimism by some about the human race, a very different and positive understanding of Jesus came along: the ideal of the "universal man" that Jesus was thought to exemplify in body, mind, and spirit. Never mind that such a Jesus is quite hard to find in the Bible.

Chapter Nine

Jesus in the Later Church

Reformations/New Worlds Era (1450–1650 CE)

Some people minded that their picture of Jesus was hard to find in the Bible. In particular, Martin Luther, an Augustinian monk and scholar living in Germany, minded. Increasingly troubled by practices of the church that were abusive (such as selling "indulgences," church certificates said to free souls from purgatory), Luther wanted to follow the Jesus of the Bible, one who was **savior** and **justifier**. Luther's Jesus was not so much the Jesus of the Gospels as the Christ of the Epistles, especially as spoken of in the letters of Paul. Paul wrote almost nothing of the historical Jesus but, even so, said he was resolved "to know nothing among you except Jesus Christ, and him crucified" (1 Cor. 2:2). Following Paul and Augustine, Luther saw Jesus as the one through whom God's grace and love had come, totally unearned by anything humans could do or say. Luther radicalized the importance of *faith*, agreeing with Paul that we are saved *sola fide* ("by faith alone"):

> Therefore, since we are justified by faith, we have peace with God through our Lord Jesus Christ, through whom we have obtained access to this grace in which we stand. . . . For while we were still weak, at the right time Christ died for the ungodly. Indeed, rarely will anyone die for a righteous person—though perhaps for a good person someone might actually dare to die. But God proves his love for us in that while we still were sinners Christ died for us. (Rom. 5:1–2, 6–8)

So Jesus the savior became for Luther, Lutherans, and Protestants generally, absolutely central. The authority of the pope (vicar of Christ), along with that of councils, was rejected in favor of the authority of Scripture and Scripture's saving Lord. Christ (formerly Pantocrator, high and harsh above the altar) began to come now from the lectern and pulpit as the **compassionate savior**. Scripture and sermon brought forth the WORD OF GOD who is Christ Jesus.

Protestants of Ulrich Zwingli and John Calvin's Reformed movement and of Henry VIII's Church of England also broke with Rome—and for a more Bible-molded Lord. As an overview of Protestantism on Jesus, historian Jaroslav Pelikan notes that a new main metaphor for Christ was used by the Reformers:

> In the characteristic phrase of Luther, Jesus was the "Mirror of the fatherly heart [of God], apart from whom we see nothing but a wrathful and terrible judge." For John Calvin likewise, "Christ is the Mirror wherein we must, and without self-deception may contemplate our own election." "Let Christ," said Calvin's Zurich colleague Heinrich Bullinger in an official confession of the Reformed Church, "be the Mirror in which we contemplate our predestination."[1]

Pelikan concludes that the Reformers interpreted the figure of Jesus, basically, as the **mirror of the Eternal**.

More than the Lutherans, Reformed, and Anglicans, the Anabaptist wing of the Protestant Reformation focused on a more human Jesus, the Jesus of the Synoptic Gospels and the Sermon on the Mount. He became **humble exemplar**. They found what Francis and the early Christians had found: a man of nonviolence who wanted the people of God's realm to be baptized out of belief, to live simply and purely, and to make no oaths, only that their yes was yes and their no, no. The Anabaptists began to make the case for *individual* discernment of who Jesus Christ was and what he meant.

The Protestant Reformation was both embarrassing and hurtful to the Roman Church. It was embarrassing because so much of what the Reformers said, Catholics knew to be true; and it was hurtful in that the unity of the church, which Rome valued, was broken even further. After several futile attempts to reign in the Reformers and their supportive princes, an ecumenical council of Catholic officials was called together in 1545–63 CE in Trent (northern Italy). They put their house in order regarding many matters of practice and belief. The prelates decided, for example, to adopt the theology of Thomas Aquinas as prescriptive and there would indeed be seven official sacraments of the church, as had been observed unofficially for several centuries. Christ became more the **Lord of the sacramental system**.

Whatever reforms Catholics mandated, they were too little, too late for northern European Christians. The Protestant-Catholic breach widened. Eventually there were wars between and among the factions, most horribly the Thirty Years' War fought in central Europe, 1618–48. In this war, Swedish forces under Gustavus Adolphus preserved Lutheran lands, and Cardinal Richelieu strengthened the hand of the French king, who forsook Huguenot Protestants in favor of Catholicism. In any and all of this, it is hard to see much of Jesus, except the one who wept over Jerusalem: "If you, even you, had only recognized on this day the things that make for peace! But now they are hidden from your eyes" (Luke 19:42).

Seemingly, those who did not stay in Europe to make war left the continent to explore the opening-up, round world. Portuguese explorers went south around Africa and east to Asia, often accompanied by Society of Jesus (Jesuit) missionaries who tried to bring the best of Catholic practice and thought to the peoples they worked among. Jesuit Matteo Ricci went to China, Francis Xavier to Japan. Founder of the Jesuits Ignatius Loyola (who had hung up his sword before the Blessed Virgin) wrote his famous *Spiritual Exercises*, which guided the new order as it went out.

Spanish explorers went west to the Americas, and, here too members of one of the religious orders usually accompanied conquistadors. The Jesus whom native peoples met usually was the militant **Christus Victor** (conquering Christ). He was propelled to the front when the bones of Santiago (Saint James) were "discovered" in Spain; this created a religious fervor that put a "General Jesus" into action against the Moors and Jews in Spain and for conversion of native populations of Nueva España across the Atlantic. So Christus Victor came.

The Christ with whom native peoples could identify, however, was **Christus Victus**, the crucified Lord. The suffering God has had powerful appeal to subjugated people, from our ancestors in Egypt, in Babylon, and under the Greeks and Romans, to peasants and serfs and, now in the 1500s, colonized natives and enslaved Africans. The statement about Christ that "he knew exactly the life we know" has been of comfort to those who have known the lance and the lash. By 1540 native people in what would one day be the United States, such as New Mexico, experienced Jesus as victor and victim.

To the New World there also came people who wanted to move away from Europe, resettle, and build communities on religious principles. One famous group was the Pilgrims who came to New England to plant and to worship. As they left Holland (having first fled England), their Pastor John Robinson said, "Remember, God has yet more light and truth to break forth from his Holy Word." As Protestants devoted to the Bible ("the cradle in which Christ is rocked," Luther said), these New World pioneers believed that "something new" might break forth. There was, then, in these early pioneers, an appreciation of **Christ of the open way**, the Christ who said in the book of Revelation, "See, I am making all things new" (Rev. 21:5). Christians living in North America effectively operated with a Lord who beckoned followers forward. They responded to Paul's words, "[F]orgetting what lies behind and straining forward to what lies ahead, I press on toward the goal for the prize of the heavenly call of God in Christ Jesus" (Phil. 3:13–14).

As history went into modern times, awareness of the globe and its people continued to move Christians to take the gospel "into all the world." Already present in Catholic missionary efforts, a **sending Christ** came to the fore for Protestants in nineteenth-century Europe and the United States. Christ's evangelistic work has continued into the twentieth and twenty-first centuries. In time, Jesus no longer looked Caucasian but was of many hues and facial contours and had more followers in Latin America, Africa, and Asia than in Europe and North America.

The Ecumenical Age (1650 CE–Present)

All that Jesus has been and become through four millennia probably still exists in the world. There is still the powerful Christ Pantocrator in Orthodox churches. There is still the humble Servant ministering in forgotten places. And, in between, there are many other Jesuses. In recent centuries the Jesus whom people in the West seem to know best is one who is **the individual**. This projected Jesus tends to be self-made, personal, feeling-related, antiauthoritarian, and psychological—to name a few, not altogether compatible, attributes.

Following the sense of new freedom in Christ let loose by the Protestant Reformation, there soon followed a restricting reaction in Lutheran and Reformed circles, a veritable hardening of theological thought, with considerable moral rigidity. Catholics too made Thomas Aquinas's theology the orthodox norm to which believers were told to adhere.

Meanwhile there were new currents of thought in the wider world, most *not* related to Christianity, that would affect our understanding of Jesus. One of these forces was the rise of science, which began in earnest during the seventeenth century. The force of science has not declined a degree since. Science and scientists were not much interested in metaphysics, but rather in what could be seen and touched, verified and quantified—a "Just the facts, ma'am" approach to the world. As discoveries about the natural world were made, various "truths" of the Bible and doctrines of the church were questioned, if not refuted. Regarding Jesus, for example, the prescientific worldview did not have particular trouble believing he could walk on water, but "modern," science-influenced folk did. With the scientists they said, "If we can't replicate what he did, it likely did not happen." Jesus the miracle worker and healer took steps back in the modern world. The resurrection came in for questioning, not fitting modern criteria for credibility.

Roughly paralleling the rise of science was the Enlightenment, which extolled the power of the mind to know, to reason, and to devise intelligible systems. Reason was not dependent on revelation or under obligation to traditions, no matter how long cherished. "Man" now could become "the measure of all things," and God was not a necessary precondition except, perhaps, as the clockmaker who set things to running and then stepped back to be no more involved. A person of the Age of Reason, such as Thomas Jefferson, might admire the individual Jesus, whom he saw, and make him over without frills (no miraculous birth, attributions of divinity, miracles, or resurrection). Jefferson took the Newer Testament and cut out all that did not fit his Enlightenment worldview. *The Jefferson Bible* was a slim gospel.

So what Jesus could be in the physical world (as science allowed) and what he might be in the world of mind (as reason allowed) were diminished. But there still was wiggle room for Christianity in the world of feeling or emotions. Always there has been a **Jesus of the heart,** and this Jesus has become increasingly strong in the modern world. There arose in Protestant circles the Pietist movement, which stressed religious experience more than doctrinal assent. God was more to be found by inner stirrings. Certainly this was the case with John Wesley, a heady Anglican divine who met some Moravian Pietists on board ship from America. Moravian singing and religious fervor touched Wesley deeply. One night after his voyage, back in London at a prayer meeting, his heart "felt strangely warmed." He had a firsthand experience of the Holy. After that he began to preach with fervor and to reach women and men in a more passionate way. Methodism was born, and the emphasis that "Jesus saves" *souls* came into greater prominence. A revival began in England under John Wesley's preaching, with stirring hymns provided by his brother Charles.

In America there was the Great Awakening of the mid-1700s. Though its principal leaders, such as Jonathan Edwards, were suspicious of overt emotionalism, the Awakening granted more room for "the affections" to influence people coming to Christ. In the nineteenth century's Second Great Awakening, considerably more latitude was made for active searching, personal decision making, and letting loose in the Spirit. Manifestations in weeping, shouting, dancing, even barking, happened. In the twentieth century there was a remarkable rise in Pentecostalism with tongues-speaking and open emotional expression. The pentecostal/charismatic movement has been greatly influential in Latin America and Africa. What it says about Christ is that he is the **facilitator of the Spirit,** even as he sent the Holy Spirit at Pentecost in the first century CE.

Theological underpinning for Western Christianity's tilt toward a religion of the heart was provided by Friedrich Schleiermacher, a German theologian arguing with "religious despisers" in the early nineteenth century. His book *The Christian Religion* has had enormous intellectual influence on Christians, right to the present day. He said that "religion is the feeling of absolute dependence on God." It is *feeling*, interiority, subjectivity, opening of the heart, that is important in the religious life, not propositional or institutional or rational procedures. Jesus, as Schleiermacher understood him, was a man, **the man of God**, who grew into divinity by inward GOD CONSCIOUSNESS. Jesus kept this consciousness so perfectly as to enable him to become one with God. Schleiermacher went on to say that this man of God entrusted his mission to the church, so essential to Christian faith.

The notion of the full humanity of Jesus, his being "like us in every way," opened the door to search for **the historical Jesus**. Science (e.g., archaeology) and reason (e.g., textual criticism) spurred the belief that inquirers might truly discern the real person of the first century. Many attempts were made, and many Jesuses were found, with the seekers usually seeing their own reflection in him, as when looking down at water in a well. The image of **Jesus the teacher** had special resonance with modern, "liberal" Christians. Charles Monroe Shelton's book *In His Steps* counseled following a **moral Jesus**. The book has been a major seller from 1896 to the present day.

Some of the energy for the progressive Jesus went into what is called the social gospel movement. Social gospellers made **Jesus the reformer** prominent.

At the start of the twentieth century, Albert Schweitzer ended his quest for the historical Jesus by concluding that Jesus was an **eschatological preacher** of his day who believed that the end was near and that God would soon be breaking into history. He further suggested that Jesus hoped forfeiture of his own life might help usher in that reign of God.

There are scholars pursing the historical Jesus today who say much the same thing. Others venture to say more. Probably 100 percent of Newer Testament scholars today would agree that the historical Jesus did proclaim the Basileia of God. Many Jesus Scholars would be of a mind with Marcus Borg that Jesus (in his proclamation and life) offers us "the decisive disclosure of God."[2] Borg's Jesus is less a lawmaker or judge and more "One with whom we may be in relationship." In *Jesus at 2000* Borg offers his belief that Jesus "challenged the domination system of his day . . . was a religious ecstatic, a Jewish mystic, if you will, for whom God was an experiential reality." He concludes about the historical Jesus that he was a (1) **Spirit person**, (2) **healer**, (3) **wisdom teacher**, (4) **social prophet**, and (5) **movement initiator**.[3] That is considerably more than Schweitzer's eschatological image.

A reaction against the individual, humanistic, psychological, social activist Jesus set in during the twentieth century, initiated by another German theologian, Karl Barth. Barth took a thoughtful, revelation-affirming approach to Christ, valuing **the Christ of the creeds** as much as or more than the Jesus of history. He and the neo-orthodox theologians were wont to treat the Bible witnesses as more credible and affirm what the church through the centuries had concluded about Christ. They affirmed the historic formulations of the faith, such as the Trinity, and were quite church-centered in their theology. Barth's systematic theology was called *Church Dogmatics*.

One of the great gifts which neo-orthodoxy presented was the ecumenical movement which has helped bring Christian communions together. **Christ of the ecumenical boat** might be the image to have here, he praying "that they may all be one" (John 17:21). I have taken the liberty in this book to call the last several hundred years of the Christian story "the ecumenical age," for in many ways "the whole civilized world" is coming to see that we are all together on spaceship earth, and as Christians we are coming to see that we are called into new oneness with all humanity.

More conservative than neo-orthodox Christians has been a group of the faithful who stayed quite literalist about the Bible. They fall under the descriptor "fundamentalist" or "evangelical." Regarding Jesus, they have made belief in the virgin birth and belief in Christ's bodily resurrection two of the primary criteria for true believers.

A direction of some Western Protestant and Catholic Christians has been to see Jesus as a figure who stands over and against dominative powers. He is the one whom Jaroslav Pelikan calls **the liberator**. There is disenchantment today with regard to science and technology, economic globalization, U.S. military hegemony, consumerism, the control of mass media by the few, and strictures put on thought and people. Now comes Jesus—or Jesus' contemporary disciples—who will not capitulate to neo-conservative establishment. Jesus for them must be the one who identifies with the poor and the third world, who is in the struggle for justice and peace, who is feminist, who would reclaim the environment for all God's creatures, and who is postmodern (not slavish with regard to science, the mind, or the powers that be). This Jesus would liberate the world from all such oppressions. In that sense Jesus is also, in the words of Teilhard de Chardin, **"the Cosmic Lover,"** the one inviting faithful people forward into a new realm of being, into God's domination-free order. He is alive in a Bishop Oscar Romero, mentioned in the quotation at the beginning of this part.

Conclusion to Part 3

A generation ago, Bible scholar and mission historian Stephen Neill wrote the following:

> In Jesus Christ a force of inestimable magnitude began to operate within the world of humans. The movement that this Jesus initiated has lasted through nineteen centuries, and shows no signs of diminishing or fading. The church that bears his name has shown itself capable of sustaining the most grievous injuries, as in the Muslim invasions and the Russian Revolution. . . . It has proved able to absorb into itself many races and cultures. . . . It has taken over the most varied forms of philosophical thinking and learned to use them. . . . It has continued to inspire incomparable beauty in the fields of art and literature. No power on earth seems able to stay the cataract in which literally millions of Africans are surging into the Christian church every year. . . . The Christian church has produced a phenomenon previously unknown in the history of mankind—a universal and worldwide religion. Jesus Christ has influenced human history far more deeply than any human being of whom we have record.[4]

A similar evaluation is heard about Jesus in an unknown author's narrative description, quite poetic:

> He was born in an obscure village, the child of a peasant woman. He grew up in another obscure village, where He worked in a carpenter's

shop until He was thirty. Then for three years He was an itinerant preacher. He never had a family or owned a home. He never traveled two hundred miles from the place He was born. He never wrote a book, or held an office. He did none of the things that usually accompany greatness.

While he was still a young person, the tide of popular opinion turned against Him. His friends deserted Him. He was turned over to His enemies, and went through the mockery of a trial. He was nailed to a cross between two thieves. While he was dying, His executioners gambled for the only piece of property He had—His coat. When He was dead, He was taken down and laid in a borrowed grave.

Nineteen [now twenty] centuries have come and gone, and today He is the central figure for much of the human race. All the armies that ever marched, and all the navies that ever sailed, and all the parliaments that ever sat, and all the kings that ever reigned, put together, have not affected the life of humans upon this earth as powerfully as this **"One Solitary Life."**

Amen and Amen!

Discussion Questions for Part 3: Jesus

1. Is it legitimate to talk about Jesus *before* there ever was the child born in Bethlehem?

2. Do you agree with the author that Older Testament "predictions" of Jesus' coming are questionable but that the Scripture's ideas of Word, Spirit, and Wisdom were embodied in Christ? What was the incarnation about?

3. Is there consensus in your group about what was most important about Jesus: his birth, life, teachings, crucifixion, resurrection, something else? Many say, "His teachings." Do you agree?

4. What do you think is the "meaning" of Jesus' death? Do you lean toward Anselm, with a theory of a blood atonement, or toward Abelard, with an example theory?

5. How does Jesus have life after his historic time? In what way is Jesus "alive and well" in the twenty-first century?

Part 4

The Holy Spirit

But for me it is good to be near God.
Psalm 73:28

I will pour out my spirit on all flesh;
your sons and your daughters shall prophesy,
  your old men shall dream dreams,
  and your young men shall see visions.
Even on the male and female slaves,
  in those days, I will pour out my spirit.
Joel 2:28–29

With the mystics these experiences [of the Holy] pass up wholly
into the "over-abounding." "O that I could tell you what the heart
feels, how it burns and is consumed inwardly! Only, I find no words
to express it. I can but say: Might but one little drop of what I feel
fall into Hell, Hell would be transformed into a paradise." So says
Catherine of Genoa; and all the multitude of her spiritual kindred
testify to the same effect.
Rudolf Otto, *The Idea of the Holy*[1]

A testimony frequently heard these days is, "I'm not religious, but I have
my own spirituality." Indeed, we live in a time when spirituality is a
white-hat word, people sensing that they are not alone in the universe,
but picking their own unique way of living with the Holy. An Internet
search of amazon.com shows more than eighteen hundred volumes with
"Spirituality" in the title, as well as twelve thousand other books addressing some aspect of the same. A few years ago, sociologist Robert Bellah
did interviews to assess religiosity in America. He met a woman named

115

Sheila. Sheila said she had no need for a church or synagogue because, "I have my own faith."

"What is that?" Bellah asked.

"It's Sheilaism. Just my own little voice," she replied.[2]

Sheilaism, people relying on individual insights to guide their spiritual path, is in. Some, of course, seek supplemental help in Eastern or Native American or esoteric traditions. I believe that seekers would be aided immensely, were they to draw on the deep experience and resources of the Christian faith as a guide for the soul. Christians have had millennia of reflection on God as Holy Spirit. The Holy Spirit governs our spirituality. Especially influential have been the practices and insights of those who are mystics or persons very much like mystics.

Yet to speak about the Holy Spirit is to consider what theologian Sean Kealy calls "one of the most elusive themes in the Bible and theology."[3] We are, of course, talking about GOD, who is ever beyond categories and yet so essential to us that we cannot help but speak. For Christians to consider God-as-Spirit is especially to consider "the third person of the Trinity," a phrase that will be explored specifically in chapter 11 (p. 132ff.). I believe that God's Spirit is at work externally in the world renewing creation *and* at work internally—within people—giving a sense of the numinous that both assures and stirs to action. The elusive Spirit's history in the world with people can be told.

As we begin this discourse, the reader may find it helpful to be acquainted with meanings behind the word "S/spirit." In Hebrew the word is *ruach*; in Greek *pneuma*, as in *pneumatic*; in Latin it is *spiritus*, so that *Spiritus Sanctus* means "Holy Spirit." Hebrew, Greek, and Latin all convey the sense of "wind" and "breath." The writer of John thus can say, "The wind (*pneuma*, spirit) blows where it chooses, and you hear the sound of it, but you do not know where it comes from or where it goes" (John 3:8).

The history of the Spirit in the Bible starts at creation: "In the beginning when God created the heavens and the earth, the earth was a formless void and darkness covered the face of the deep, while a wind (*ruach*, breath-spirit) from God swept over the face of the waters" (Gen. 1:1–2). Interestingly enough, Spirit is found in the concluding verses of the Bible. Revelation 22:17 reads, "The Spirit and the bride [Christ's Church] say, 'Come.'" The Spirit, we believe, continued with people in the church throughout history, and now, in truth, there may never have been a greater time of God-the-Spirit than now. God-the-Father/Creator/Judge and God-the-Son/Incarnate/Redeemer are not as preeminent today as in some centuries of the past. Consider, then: the Spirit. Her time is now. Let us recount her moments to the present.

(Moving into this part, please note that I sometimes capitalize various ACTIONS/ATTRIBUTES/CHARACTERISTICS of the Spirit and make bold the names of **persons** who were affected by, lived in, or reflected upon Spirit significantly in our four-thousand-year story.)

Chapter Ten

The Holy Spirit in Biblical Times

Premonarchic Millennium (2000–1000 BCE)

The center of the Older Testament is the story of the exodus, our faith-parents' escape from slavery in Egypt. Their leader was the redoubtable **Moses**. Moses came to such a role with the people of Israel through a transformative SPIRITUAL EXPERIENCE. According to the book of Exodus, Moses had personally escaped Egypt and become a sheepherder with one of the tribes of the Sinai Peninsula. One day while tending his flock, he saw something incredible: a bush afire yet not burned up! He drew nearer, and God called him from out of the bush, "Moses, Moses!"

He said, "Here I am."

Told he was on holy ground, Moses took off his sandals. In the numinous encounter that followed, he learned both the name of God (Yahweh, meaning, "I am who I am" or "I will be who I will be") and what he was supposed to do with his life (lead the Hebrew slaves out of Egypt).

So he did. And our faith story began.

In addition to the burning-bush experience, Moses is remembered for a postexodus time with God. On Mount Sinai, we are told, he received the Ten Commandments. He had what theologian Rudolf Otto calls an experience of *MYSTERIUM TREMENDUM*, that is, something well beyond the ordinary, quite powerful in its effect, creating awe, and giving direction. Note some of its aspects: in SOLITUDE for forty days and nights, Moses was engulfed in CLOUDS and SMOKE on a HIGH MOUN-TAIN. Coming down from the mountain with a message, his face was SHINING with reflection of the radiance of the LIGHT of God. We shall see these and other aspects in numinous experiences of faithful men and women again in religious history.

119

Moses might be considered the first mystic, our first spiritually awakened person, one who came, as the Bible says, face to face with God (Exod. 33:11). His encounters of God in the burning bush and on Sinai were spiritually illumining and resulted in deliberate actions.

Following the exodus event and receipt of the Ten Commandments came forty years of disciplined wandering in the Sinai Desert. Finally, the former slaves entered the promised land of Canaan. Moses, however, did not come with them. Instead, he viewed the people's entrance from atop Mount Nebo on the east side of the Jordan River. That is the last we hear of him. Legend has it that he was never buried, as no one knew his grave site. Instead, he was left free to wander the hills. As such, according to tradition, he could appear in subsequent religious encounters, as to Jesus 1300 years later on the mount of transfiguration! That is something of his posthistorical story.

There is also pre-Moses material involving the Spirit to consider. We are told in Genesis that Moses' precursors, the early patriarchs and matriarchs in the faith, had notable spiritual experiences. Consider the first quasi-historical character of the Bible: Abram who would become **Abraham**. Abram was told to leave his country of origin in distant Babylon and go to a place God would show him. He and wife Sarai went by DREAMS received. Abraham, often called the father of faith, is forever considered a person open and attentive to God. He and Sarai, for example, met and showed hospitality to three strangers who visited them at their desert home (see Gen. 18 for details), and in that process they encountered the Holy. They received a blessed announcement that Sarai's barrenness would end. Her name was changed to **Sarah**.

Abraham and Sarah's son was **Isaac**, and Genesis 24:63 includes a phrase of significance for this chapter. It says Isaac "went out to meditate in the field in the evening" (RSV). The phrase is almost a throwaway, as though MEDITATION were a regular discipline in his life. On one such evening's meditation, during a walk in the field, he looked out and saw a woman riding toward him on a camel. She became his soul mate, Rebekah, whom he married and loved.

Isaac and Rebekah's son, **Jacob** (later renamed Israel, meaning "He who strives with God"), really picked up the divine-encounter pace. One night at Bethel ("house of God"), he had the vision of a ladder to heaven on which angels were ascending and descending. Another time, at Peniel ("face of God"), he wrestled all night with a man/demon/God until he received that Other's blessing—as well as a wound to his hip. We have with Jacob's encounters more components of spiritual experience: SACRED

PLACE, DARKNESS, VISION (face of God), DIVINE BEINGS, STRUGGLE, BLESSINGS, and SUFFERING. These we shall see time and again through history. Jacob's struggle and suffering speak to the spiritual idea of the DARK NIGHT OF THE SOUL.

Another great pre-Mosaic figure is **Joseph,** credited with saving his people from starvation and responsible for getting them into Egypt, thus setting up the exodus five hundred years later. Joseph was a dreamer and an interpreter of dreams, reminding us that DREAMS play an important role in much spirituality. For one thing, they often issue forth in prophecy, which is speech and/or action and/or discerning (predicting) what shall happen. Prophets will be understood as operating under the Spirit.

Moving back to Moses' time and the years immediately following, we encounter **Joshua** and some leaders known as judges. Their stories are told in the Older Testament books of Joshua and Judges. The writers of these books say that the heroes and heroines of Israel were under the influence of the Holy Spirit too, though in a slightly different way. Here the Spirit was the one who seemed to pick people like **Othniel, Gideon,** and **Deborah** for leadership positions. They were infused with CHARISMA or power to lead the people in military victory against their enemies. Here was ENTHUSIASM, meaning "God (*Theo*) is inside." It was one aspect of what the Spirit of God might create.

The Spirit would also anoint a prophet who, in turn, would anoint a king.

Time of the Kings and the Prophets (1000–550 BCE)

One such prophet was **Samuel**. Samuel had profound religious direction from the time of his boyhood. As a youth serving in the temple, he heard the word of the Lord in the SILENCE of the night and followed the instructions received. He was a person inwardly attuned and outwardly involved, both a contemplative and an activist. He anointed **Saul** to be Israel's first king.

One of the things that happened to Saul, not atypical of Spirit-leading, was an encounter that led to verbal and physical expression. On the road after his coronation Saul met a band of prophets. They were possessed of the Spirit that, in turn, affected him (see 1 Sam. 10:9–13). Saul went into a PROPHETIC FRENZY. He was "carried away," every bit as much as Spirit-filled Pentecostals today. Not for this reason, but because of his paranoia and lack of success on the battlefield, Saul was, sadly, not adequate to the job of king.

Samuel then received instruction to anoint another person to replace

Saul. He anointed **David.** The anointing then (and now) involved a laying on of hands and investing the anointed with the blessing of God's Spirit. David, in our accounts, became the king nonpareil. In the Older Testament he was second only to Moses in importance, and he had a deeply spiritual side to him. Consider some of his characteristics. PRAYER was a primary dimension to his spirituality. The book of Psalms is attributed to his authorship, and no writing more spiritual is known. People are still meditating on David's eight-word prayer "Be still, and know that I am God!" (Ps. 46:10). The Bible also indicates that David was skilled at playing the harp, and we know that MUSIC plays a huge part in the holy life. David is also described as the "prince of mourners," one who knew TEARS for his sins and in the face of life's tragedies; yet he was one who could "DANCE before the Lord"—perhaps naked (see 2 Sam. 6). In all, he is a marvelous example of one who demonstrated depth of soul despair and height of spirit soaring. In time, Jesus would be called "the son of David" for many look-alike reasons (anointedness, prayer, tears, etc.).

David's crowning achievements are two: he united the twelve disparate tribes of Israel, and he established Jerusalem as the nation's capital. Jerusalem means, literally, "city of peace," and though it has known mostly war for three thousand years, Zion is considered HOLY GROUND, a "thin place," if you will, where God's Spirit may break through.

In Jerusalem, David's son **Solomon** built a temple. It especially came to be considered SACRED EDIFICE, where human-divine encounter could happen—even as it might in churches. Christians say yet at the start of worship, "The LORD is in his holy temple; let all the earth keep silence before him!" (Hab. 2:20). There were, of course, other sacred shrines to be found among the Hebrews, at Bethel, Shechem, and Dan, but for those authors who finally assembled the Older Testament, there was no greater place than Jerusalem and its temple. The Holy of Holies in the temple held Israel's sacred objects: the stone tablets with the Ten Commandments, encased in an arcadia wood box called the ark of the covenant. It was believed that Yahweh's Spirit hovered over the ark. So sacred were this place and these artifacts that only the highest ranking priest could enter—and then only once a year! CANDLES (the delight of persons of every spiritual age) were on stands there.

During the eighth century BCE in the Holy of Holies the prophet **Isaiah of Jerusalem** had a life-changing experience. One can read about it in Isaiah 6. His EPIPHANY ("appearance, manifestation of the holy") contained fire, smoke, angels, voices, confession, obliteration, and, especially, awareness of Yahweh's holiness. This was a *mysterium tremendum* experience of awe at the majesty of the divine Other. Words cannot describe what happened, but words are still employed, to hint at the meaning of numinous events. So it was for Isaiah. In his experience he received both theological content (understanding of God's holiness) and action-direction. The people were to return to doing justice, or they would come to destruction. Rudolf Otto contends that moral directive often accompanies spiritual experience.[1]

One of the principal figures calling for righteousness in the ninth century BCE was the prophet **Elijah**. He was of the northern kingdom of Israel—which, after Solomon's time, had separated from the southern kingdom of Judah. Elijah came to be considered the greatest of the prophets. His greatness and contribution to the mystical path comes from the time he was forced to flee from the wrath of Queen Jezebel and take refuge in a cave on a mountain ("cave" for going inward and "mountain" for gaining vision). From the cave Elijah looked for God's appearance. There was an earthquake, but God was not in it. There was a rush of fire, perhaps lightning, but God was not in that. There was thunder, but God was not there. Finally, Elijah hunkered down and wrapped his mantle about himself, and God spoke in "a sound of sheer silence" (1 Kgs. 19:12). Not in a grand outward event, but in this SILENCE OF SOLITUDE, "a still small voice" (RSV) was heard, the Holy One was made known, and direction was given.

Israel, with its capital Samaria, came to a bloody end by the Assyrians' sword in 722 BCE. The ten tribes of the northern kingdom were "lost" from history. The southern kingdom, whose capital was Jerusalem, held out a bit longer, till 586 BCE. Then it fell and its leading citizens were force-marched east to Babylon.

A witness *to* the fall of Jerusalem, as well as a witness *for* Yahweh before and during the fall, was the prophet **Jeremiah**. He was a man of immense spiritual sensitivity, capable of profound lamentation *and* of undying hope. His most famous words are ones to gladden the despairing soul:

> The days are surely coming, says the LORD, when I will make a new covenant with the house of Israel and the house of Judah. . . . I will put my law within them, and I will write it on their hearts [INTE-RIORITY]; and I will be their God, and they shall be my people. No longer shall they teach one another, or say to each other, "Know the LORD," for they shall all know me [UNION], from the least of them to the greatest, says the LORD. (Jer. 31:31–34)

Of similar hopeful word was **Ezekiel**. He knew the deep agony of the people of Judah captive in Babylon. In his VISION of restitution there was a valley of dried bones (the hopeless people), but the bones came together. They were given flesh, and, finally, God breathed life into them. Life came by the breath-wind-*ruach*-Spirit!

Second Temple Period (550–20 BCE)

Jeremiah's prophecy and Ezekiel's hope of restoration for the captives were realized through one who was ANOINTED by the Spirit, but who was not a believer in Yahweh. In 538 BCE, King **Cyrus the Persian**, who by then had conquered the Babylonians, allowed captive peoples to return to their places of origin. So the remnant Jews (of Jerusalem, *Ju*dea) went home to take up their lives again. Remembering their holy ground, they rebuilt the walls of the city. Recalling their sacred edifice, they put up a new temple, the Second Temple. And knowing they were a people governed by a God who acts in history, they assembled a SACRED TEXT, first known and loved as the Law (Genesis, Exodus, Leviticus, Numbers, and Deuteronomy).

To the Law would be added, in time, the Prophets (some of the people we've heard from already, along with other inspired voices, such as Third Isaiah, Jonah, and Daniel). To the Law and the Prophets would come what are called the Writings, most notably the Psalms, Proverbs, and Song of Solomon. All the material taken together would make up the Bible (that is, "collection of books") that Christians designate as the Older Testament. By and large, Jews and Christians have considered all these writings to be, in some sense, INSPIRED by God, God's Spirit writ large in them.

While these books have myth, story and legend, history and quasi-history, law codes and genealogies, commentary-judgment-predictions, counsel on living, poetry, and more in them, they can be deeply spiritual. Often they speak to the heart and soul of their readers. The Psalms come to mind first in this regard. They have praise, lamentation, thanksgiving, confession, and more in them. For our purposes in this chapter, we should emphasize that they are filled with DESIRE for God, as Psalm 42:1–2 illustrates:

> As a deer longs for flowing streams,
>   so my soul longs for you, O God.
> My soul thirsts for God,
>   for the living God.

When shall I come and behold
    the face of God?

Such desire is at the heart of every contemplative. There were persons who so longed 2,500 years ago, as there are such persons today.

The book of this period that receives greatest attention among mystics-as-seekers-of-God more than two millennia later is the Song of Solomon. Ostensibly this is man-woman love poetry, but spiritually sensitive interpreters have always given this poetry divine-human interpretation: we long for God, as God desires us too. Consider:

I am my beloved's,
    and his desire is for me.
Come, my beloved,
    let us go forth into the fields,
    and lodge in the villages;
let us go out early to the vineyards,
    and see whether the vines have budded,
whether the grape blossoms have opened
    and the pomegranates are in bloom.
There I will give you my love.
Song 7:10–12

The writer of the Song and later interpreters find LOVE to be the bond between God and people, Yahweh and Israel, Christ and the church, or "The Spirit and me." This is a profoundly spiritual book!

The creation of sacred Scripture is unquestionably the most important religious thing to happen in the five hundred years of the Second Temple Period. Such text provides the inspiring encounter-with-God stories of patriarchs, prophets, and people. Knowing past struggles and celebrations in God provided clues to other generations for their own time. In the late-written book of Daniel is a line demonstrating a religious practice that is still observed: DISCIPLINED PRAYER. When **Daniel** was confronted with a document from the king that would take away his life and that of his people, the Bible says that

he continued to go to his house, which had windows in its upper room open toward Jerusalem, and to get down on his knees three times a day to pray to his God and praise him, just as he had done previously. (Dan. 6:10)

The operative idea here is "as he had done previously." So discipline—even what later monks and nuns would call "hours"—is early on observed.

The major political problem facing our ancestors during the five hundred years before Christ was how to live under domination by others. They had indeed returned from exile in Babylon, but the Persians exercised suzerainty over them for two hundred years. Then in the 330s BCE, Alexander of Macedonia came onto the scene conquering, and the Greeks ruled.

Greek political and cultural domination had enormous consequences. Consider, first, the Greek influence on understanding God. Whereas the Hebrew people previously related to God primarily in terms of God's actions, the Greeks were more philosophical, wanting to ask about God's nature and attributes. One of God's attributes that the Greeks greatly valued was WISDOM or *Sophia*. Jews living in the Diaspora (dispersion) tried to bring Yahweh and Sophia into some harmony and concluded that Wisdom was of God. Wisdom was considered as existing from "the beginning." Her ways were to be walked in. In the wisdom literature the writers of Proverbs and Ecclesiastes extol the faithful to get a heart of wisdom and to live in fear (AWE) of the Lord. Sophia calls out in Proverbs 9:4–6,

> "You that are simple, turn in here!"
>   To those without sense she says,
> "Come, eat of my bread
>   and drink of the wine I have mixed.
> Lay aside immaturity, and live,
>   and walk in the way of insight."

In the book of Wisdom (included in some Bibles) 10:15, 17–19, faith history is retold with feminine pronouns:

> A holy people and blameless race
> wisdom delivered from a nation of oppressors . . .
> [S]he guided them along a marvelous way,
> and became a shelter to them by day,
> and a starry flame through the night.
> She brought them over the Red Sea,
> and led them through deep waters;
> but she drowned their enemies,
> and cast them up from the depth of the sea.

This remembrance of God's femininity is included to be sure that we do not talk about God in masculine pronouns all the time and to encourage the spiritual journey within Christian circles with God's distaff nature enlivening the faithful. This is part of our legacy from Greek cultural influence reworked in the faith.

In the second century BCE one of the Greek rulers over Palestine, Antiochus IV Epiphanes, entered the temple in Jerusalem and desecrated it, installing there a statue of a foreign deity. Around 160 BCE an armed revolt, the Maccabean revolt, began against the Greek overlords. As with the judges and others earlier, the leaders of this revolt were considered to be anointed and empowered by God's Spirit. Amazingly enough, the revolt succeeded and produced a historical window of relative autonomy for Judea. One hundred years later, the Romans arrived to dominate Palestine. It was but a few decades until the man of Nazareth, called Jesus, was born.

Newer Testament Times (20 BCE–110 CE)

Jesus was a "Spirit Person." That is the first descriptor which Newer Testament scholar Marcus Borg gives Jesus. "Spirit Person" is his

> phrase for a person who has frequent and vivid experiences of the sacred, of God, of the Spirit. Such people are religious ecstatics who in nonordinary states of consciousness have experiences that seem overwhelmingly to them to be experiences of the sacred, of God.[2]

Jesus' closeness to God led his followers, then and now, to conclude that he was Emmanuel ("God with us"), the anointed/messiah/Christ of God, the Son of God. There are at least three events in the telling of Jesus' life where God's presence with Jesus is evident in a most Spirit-ual way.

One is at his baptism in the River Jordan. According to Mark's Gospel (1:10), when Jesus came out of the water, the Spirit of God, "like a DOVE" (ever the sign of the Holy Spirit) came upon him. Jesus heard a voice that said, "You are my Son, the Beloved; with you I am well pleased" (Mark 1:11). Such an experience must have been both confirming and empowering. Jesus was then enabled to go about the business of teaching, preaching, healing, praying, living, and confronting for what he called the Basileia or reign of God. His person, experiences, teachings, and work made him a most charismatic person, drawing men, women, and children to him. The God whom Jesus knew and spoke of was one whose name was to be "hallowed" (kept holy) and whose nature, more than anything else, was forgiving and loving. It was and would be LOVE, more than any other aspect of God, that in subsequent centuries contemplatives would use to talk about the divine-human connection.

The second major luminous event in Jesus' life took place on Mount Hermon in Lebanon. (Some traditions say it was Mount Tabor in southern Galilee.) Jesus ascended the mountain with his closest disciples and there, in the midst of a covering cloud, was mystically joined by Moses and Elijah, two great Spirit-directed figures whom we have previously met. Again God's reassuring voice was heard: "This is my Son, the Beloved; listen to him!" (Mark 9:7). On the mountain he was transfigured; his face and clothes glowed with the radiance of God.

At this turning point in his life, Jesus left the area of Galilee in the north of Palestine and "set his face" to go to Jerusalem. In Jerusalem, on the night of a last supper with his disciples, he had a third major spiritual experience, one of descent. He believed he was going to be killed and that it might even be God's will. So he prayed to his Father that the cup (death) might pass from him. This time there was no voice of God, only Jesus' lonely passion. God was SILENT. It was a DARK NIGHT OF THE SOUL in which the ABSENCE of God was felt, though God still was.

Jesus was in fact arrested and tried as a blasphemer against God and as a leader of sedition against the Roman state. He was convicted, whipped, and finally crucified. Rudolf Otto says that the cross is the greatest demonstration of the *mysterium* of God that ever has been. Nothing made sense in the crucifixion in any rational way, but, in God, all was received and resolved—even though Jesus, his disciples, and the world could not understand it at the time. Even so, Jesus went to his death trusting. He said, according to Luke 23:46, "Father, into your hands I commend my spirit." His spirit was committed to God, even as God's Spirit assuredly had been in him.

God, we believe, had a surprise for all: the resurrection of Jesus!

Mysteriously, unexplainably, on the third day after his death, the tomb in which he was buried was empty. Jesus' physical body was gone . . . and, then, his "spiritual body" (Paul's descriptor in 1 Cor. 15) was with the disciples again. He redirected them into mission for the reign of God on earth and promised them additional spiritual support.

Such support came on the day of Pentecost, fifty days after Passover. Then Jesus' followers received the BAPTISM OF THE HOLY SPIRIT, confirming them and empowering them, every bit as much as the Spirit earlier had done for Jesus. They were anointed by TONGUES OF FIRE (a great symbol of the Holy Spirit) that rested on their heads, and they also were given the GIFT OF TONGUES, ability to communicate in other languages. What happened on Pentecost in that upper room in Jerusalem reenthused them. They were ready to go "to the ends of the earth" (Acts 1:8) with Christ's gospel. They bore the good news of Christ Jesus to Rome, capital city of the empire. Looking back, we conclude that the world was being changed by those disciple-apostles. Anthropologist Margaret Mead could have had Jesus' followers in mind when she said, "Never doubt that a small group of thoughtful, committed individuals can change the world; indeed, it is the only thing that ever has!"

The signs and wonders the apostles did, the witness they bore, the trials they suffered, and the story of the Spirit who accompanied them are all told in the book the Acts of the Apostles. That book could just as well be called the Acts of the Holy Spirit, as God's Spirit was ever active. It came to **Peter** in a DREAM (which opened him to non-Jewish Gentiles) and to **Paul** and **Silas** in a SONG (which worked to free them from jail). Dip into Acts anywhere and the power of the Spirit is proclaimed.

In his letters to various churches and individuals, Paul of Tarsus, just mentioned, wrote something that has deepened Christian spirituality for all time. Some 164 times in his surviving writings, he talks about being "in Christ" or "in the Spirit." Nobody really knows what this phrase means—as definition must be fuzzy with matters so overwhelming—but Paul was convinced that God was in Christ and that he, Paul, was in the Lord too. What later mystics call UNION is involved in such reflections. Charles Williams, who wrote a history on the Holy Spirit, thinks that CO-INHERENCE is what happens. Co-inherence (exchange and conversion, mutual interpenetration) happens between God the Father, Son, and Holy Spirit, between God and people, and between and among people. It is, Williams says, "the very pattern of Christianity."[3]

One of the things that makes co-inherence possible is PRAYER. Prayer was certainly central to Jesus' life and is presented in the Newer Testament as a way of holiness. Harry Emerson Fosdick says that

> personal prayer became the typical message of divine fellowship. Men were to pray "without ceasing" and "in every place." Indeed, the New Testament lives and moves and has its being in the atmosphere of informal, unconventional, spontaneous, intimate prayer.[4]

Later we shall investigate various modes of prayer, but the point here is that prayer has been definitive to the faith for those who would be "spirit persons" with Jesus.

As the first century CE came to conclusion, the evangelist **John** reflected on the Spirit in his Gospel. That Gospel is a meditative, symbolic, high-soaring, mystical presentation of Jesus' life, death, and resurrection. John began by saying, "In the beginning was the Word." The Word, John proclaimed, entered into the world in Christ Jesus, illumining the darkness. LIGHT is ever the property of God's Spirit. Later, in the middle of his Gospel, John reported Jesus saying, "The Father and I are one" (John 10:30). This is the idea of co-inherence, or union, mentioned above. Finally, at the end of the Gospel, another absolutely critical element was added. Jesus said that after he was gone, the Father would send "another ADVOCATE" (John 14:16) to be with his people. This Advocate, sometimes called Helper or Comforter, is known in the Greek as the Paraclete. The Advocate is not quite the same as the Holy Spirit and yet functions in such way as to be joined. John called the Paraclete "the Spirit of truth" (John 16:13), who would guide the faithful into all the truth. The early church and subsequent generations of the faithful were indeed comforted and inspired by the active presence of Christ's Advocate (Spirit of truth) in the Holy Spirit.

Chapter Eleven

The Holy Spirit in the Early Church

Struggling Centuries of the Church (110–500 CE)

Christians of the first and even second generation believed that Jesus would be coming back soon, within their lifetime. Fervently they prayed the *Maranatha* prayer, "Come, Lord Jesus!" (Rev. 22:20). When Christ did not return quickly, they began to understand that his return had already taken place by way of the Spirit or Advocate, as discussed above. In theological language, this is *realized eschatology*, meaning, that the expected "last things" have already come to pass. Jesus' coming had happened. He was present in the Spirit. The church that was coming into being, therefore, saw itself as Spirit-led.

What the Spirit suggested to many was that, to be faithful, they needed to continue to confess that Jesus is Lord. Such confession, though, might draw them into disfavor with established religious and political authority. They might be called to suffer and die with Christ. For his confession of faith, a young man named **Stephen** was stoned to death, becoming the first martyr or witness. As Stephen was dying, he prayed that the Lord would receive his spirit (Acts 7:59). By tradition, martyrdom also happened to Paul, Peter, and all the other original disciples, save John the beloved.

To say Jesus is Lord was tantamount to saying who was *not* Lord, namely, Caesar. And if a caesar concluded he himself was a god—as caesars began to do—then most Christians could not bend the knee to him or put the pinch of incense on coals before his bust. So it was that during the first centuries of the Common Era many of the faithful came to join Christ in suffering and death. Those who were arrested, tortured, and killed felt that the Spirit of Christ was with them. **Felicitas**, a slave girl in

Carthage in the early 200s, felt so supported. While in prison, she bore a child. In pain she screamed. Her pagan jailers asked her, "If you shriek at *that*, how do you expect to endure death by the beasts?"

She replied, "Now *I* suffer what *I* suffer; then another will be in me who will suffer with me, as I shall suffer for him."

In a sentence Felicitas offered excellent definition of Christian faith, by the concept mentioned in the last chapter: CO-INHERENCE. Christ/the Spirit inhered with her, she suggested, as she inhered in Christ/the Spirit. Charles Williams comments that by her statement "Felicitas took her place for ever among the great African doctors of the Universal Church."[1]

So there were martyr witnesses, and there were writing witnesses who tried to make the faith make sense in the Greco-Roman world. Also led by the Spirit, they became apologists (explainers) for the faith. Intellectual depth was generated by **Clement of Alexander** and his successor, **Origen**, in the early third century. As students of Greek culture, they claimed that the best of Greek thought about God was compatible with the Bible and with Christ. Plato, for example, had spoken regarding the ideal forms. Such forms, the apologists said, belonged to God, who is ineffable mystery, but a mystery into which one may enter. What is needed, Clement said, is *gnosis* ("knowing") and illumination, provided by Christ and made accessible by Scripture, which could lead to UNION with God. Origen spoke of two ways for Christians to follow: the way of the crucified Christ (see Felicitas, mentioned above) and the way of perfection, which involved CONTEMPLATION of the Word dwelling in the Father. Clement and Origen are considered the founders of Christian mysticism.

Many worked in these centuries to reconcile philosophy and theology. A most important task was to agree upon doctrine regarding God. That could happen in 325 CE, when the Emperor Constantine (who had ended persecution) gathered Christian bishops to Nicaea (located in today's northwest Turkey). The bishops devised a *credo* ("I believe") statement regarding the nature of God as Trinity. "Trinity" was a concept of the Divine formed first by the Latin-speaking **Tertullian**. He said there was one God but in three persons (or masks): *Pater, Filius, et Spiritus Sanctus.* Such an idea became the framework for the Nicene Creed and the touchstone for orthodoxy ("right belief"). The HOLY SPIRIT (third person) was incorporated into the Godhead as "consubstantial, coequal, coeternal" with the Father and the Son. When speaking of the Holy Spirit, then, one was speaking of God. In time, the Western, or Roman Catholic,

Church would focus somewhat more on the oneness of God, while the Eastern, or Greek Orthodox, Church would remember the uniqueness of each person in the Godhead. The East, then, perhaps understood the Spirit better than the West.

Not everyone agreed with the decisions about the Holy Spirit. A group called the Pneumatomachi denied the full divinity of the Spirit. **Basil the Great**, one of the Cappadocian Fathers of Asia Minor, countered the Pneumatomachi in a piece called *On the Holy Spirit*, saying the Spirit was present with God in creation and had the assignment of "perfecting" creation. Basil's theological interpretation carried the day, so that any diminution of the Spirit by any group or individual was stopped at the Council of Constantinople in 381 CE. Then the Holy Spirit was reaffirmed with full standing within the Godhead. It should be noted, however, that the Holy Spirit is given limited wordage in most creedal formulations. In the Nicene Creed, for example, the Spirit receives four descriptive phrases and the Son twenty! There was more controversy about the incarnate God than over the spiritual God.

When persecution of Christians ended, what the most devout did, so as to be able to identify with Christ and be "in Christ," was follow the UNION route suggested by Clement and Origen. They could do so by *voluntarily* entering into the suffering of Christ. Asceticism, already present in the third century, really took off in the new era of Constantinian toleration. Monasticism (male and female) was born, taking two forms, that of the solitary monk and that of those gathered in community. **Paul of Thebes** and **Antony of the Desert** were solitaries. **Pachomius**, who founded nine monasteries and two convents, was a communitarian. Whether monks were alone in the wilderness or cloistered in an urban compound, they sought by prayer and fasting to attain to God, to co-inhere. This was not mysticism per se, like that which came later, but it was the major building block for that form of spirituality.

In the Eastern church a rule for structure and ethos of the monasteries was established by **Basil of Caesarea** (in Asia Minor) around the year 400. A little more than a century later, **Benedict of Nursia** (in Italy) did the same for the Western church. These Eastern and Western rules are, for the most part, still observed today. At the heart of Benedictine communities is the *opus Dei* ("work of God"), which centers in observing the divine office or hours, with daily routine of worship with Scripture readings (*lectio divina*) and prayer. Guided by this manual, manuscript copying, meals, sleep, study, communal worship, and private prayer of a monk's or nun's day took shape.

Greatly influencing Christian thought on the Holy Spirit was the theological giant **Augustine**, bishop of Hippo (North Africa, 354–430 CE), often titled the prince of mystics. Three of Augustine's thoughtful contributions to Christian spirituality may be mentioned. First, he talked about *VISIO DEI* ("vision of God"), the idea that "to go within is to go above." Certainly the idea of God at the center of one's being is ever the way the mystically faithful understand God. Second, Augustine spoke of *IMAGO DEI* ("image of God"), which has it that each person is a mirror of the Trinity, each of us being spirit-body-soul yet one. Third, Augustine spoke of *MEDIATOR DEI ET HOMINUM* ("the mediator between God and humans"); the mediator is Christ and Christ's church. In practical terms, Christian spirituality functions within the container of community. We are related to one another, accepting spiritual direction from others who assist with inner deepening. There may be hermits who live isolated spiritual lives, but by and large Christian spirituality is practiced in community, in great measure because the prince of mystics, Augustine, defined it so.

As far as mysticism proper is concerned, the other influential giant of this time was **Dionysius the Pseudo-Areopagite**, an unknown late-fifth-century CE monk, probably from Syria. His name is borrowed from that of the Dionysius mentioned in Acts 17:34. In *Mystical Theology* Dionysius described three "ways" of the spiritual life: PURGATION, ILLUMINATION, and UNION. People who walk labyrinths today understand the ways: (1) "walking in" purgation (casting off of sin, concerns, and thought); (2) "resting" in the center, illumination (receiving presence and insight as a gift); and (3) "walking out," being in a unitive state with God and humanity. Dionysius's greatest contribution was the third, the idea of union with God, or perfection, or what he also called "deification." Union is possible, he suggested, by a process of "unknowing." This involves contemplation, which leaves behind both the senses and the intellect; so the soul enters into a kind of obscurity—or "cloud," if you will—that one may be illumined by a "ray of divine darkness."

This is what a friend calls "woo-woo stuff," albeit from a long time ago! Someone interested in spiritual growth, though, could well work with the likes of Dionysius for deepening into God.

The Age of Monasticism (500–1100 CE)

The spiritual deepening, theological enlightenment, and strong acceptance of Christian faith so promising in the first half of the first millennium CE were considerably upset in the next five hundred years. This was especially so in western Europe and for what was increasingly the Roman Catholic Church. For the Germanic (some call them "barbarian") people who came into the empire from the north and east, the learnings of Western civilization and the faith of Christians were not important. Rome was sacked in 410 CE—and several times more by invading armies. The great libraries of western Europe were burned. Churches and monasteries were torn down. In desperation during the onslaught, manuscripts and holy books were shipped off to one of the few places the invaders had not overrun: Ireland.

Ireland received the faith from **Patrick** in the fifth century. Left alone by Rome, Celtic monks developed some unique practices, including emphasis on penance (with rigors and asceticism), appreciation of nature in the spiritual life, and acceptance of the hermit monk. With a passion for learning, the Irish copied manuscripts and observed *LECTIO DIVINA* (holy reading) in their communal life. To hear, "Be still, and know that I am God!" (Ps. 46:10)—and then be still—was to open oneself to the possibility of closer relationship to God. Irish Christianity, then, was mystical, knowing the depths of prayer.

The Irish monks also were not afraid of work, and in the year 564 CE missionaries began to work on winning Europe back to the faith. They went east to Scotland, Wales, England, France, and, really, everywhere from Iceland to North Africa to Russia. Their version of Christianity was based less on hierarchy (diocesan bishops, etc.) than on the monastic model, with greater separation from the world. Monasteries and convents became islands of holiness to model faith, learning, and work in a pagan sea. They would attract converts to their way and slowly win back the world.

One particular Celtic monk was of immense influence: **Duns Scotus** (meaning "Scot") **Erigena**. This scholar of the ninth century in France translated Dionysius's *Mystical Theology* from Greek into Latin and thus offered CONTEMPLATIVE PRAYER to the West. The later monks of France, Cluniacs and Cistercians, would vitalize and spread the life of deep prayer again into Western Christendom. They followed the Rule of Benedict and kept solid the monastic/convent base for mysticism.

Frankish kings played the major political role in stabilizing the West. It began in the eighth century when Charles Martel defeated Saracen (Arab) Muslims who had come into southern France. Martel's grandson, Charles, expanded the Frankish realm considerably and became head of a new Holy Roman Empire on Christmas Day, 800 CE, crowned by the pope. Called **Charlemagne**, he was for this period and for Western Christianity what Constantine had been five hundred years earlier and what Cyrus had been eight hundred years before Constantine—a savior, a messiah, one ANOINTED. He began the process of reunifying Europe, and he did so in terms of Catholic Christianity. Monasteries and convents were encouraged, along with the Carolingian (Charles's) Renaissance of educational and cultural advance. Palace schools were often attached to monasteries; so faith and learning went side by side.

With mention above of Saracen Muslims, we need to look east again. The Byzantine portion of the old Roman Empire was, for the most part, spared the destructive onslaught of the Germanic invasions. So Constantinople and Orthodoxy fared reasonably well in the fifth and sixth centuries, flourishing under the Emperor Justinian in the sixth century. Within the Eastern Church, though, there was internal division over beliefs and practices. Christians of Syria and Egypt tended toward monophysitism, which emphasized Christ's oneness of divinity, at the expense of his full humanity. They became increasingly alienated from their Aegean area Orthodox coreligionists.

So when the armies of Islam came riding out of the Arabian deserts, conquering for Allah in the early seventh century, the non-Orthodox Christians of the Middle East and North Africa said, "Welcome!" They perceived their lot would be better under the Islamic Arabs than the Orthodox Byzantines. Over the centuries, though, second-class religious status and attrition would wear down their vitality so that today such Christians are a small minority.

The Eastern Orthodox Church stayed less engaged in affairs of state than its Western church counterpart. This was due in large measure because the emperor himself was right there in Constantinople and able to control the clergy. The Catholic Church of the West, not as much under the eye of the emperor, was able to exercise itself in the public arena more freely. This helps account for some difference between the Orthodox and Catholic churches over time.

Even so, both branches emphasized and made Communion the central religious ritual of the faith, Orthodoxy emphasizing the DIVINE MYSTERY OF THE EUCHARIST all the more. The Orthodox began to put up a screen with icons on it (which the faithful could revere). Behind that iconostasis, or screen, the changing of the bread and wine into Christ's body and blood took place, increasing the mystery of the action. Orthodoxy was early to use candles and smoke-producing incense in the Divine Liturgy, all of which said, "Holy, Holy, Holy" to worshippers. The East also put greater emphasis on the resurrection of Christ and on God's transcendent GLORY. The total effect, which constituted an increase in the sense of the *mysterium tremendum* and otherworldliness, has made for a distinctive spirituality.

The Eastern Church's religious depth was carried by monks and nuns every bit as much as in the West. Two sacred places, each a center for monasticism, stand out as of great importance then and now: Mount Athos, a peninsula in Greece, and the caves of Cappadocia in Turkey. Led by **Simeon the New Theologian** of the tenth century, Eastern religious folk believed that, in contemplation, they came into the VERY PRESENCE of God. **Barlaam the Calabrian**, a humanist Orthodox monk, countered such argument, saying that one comes face to face with God only in the afterlife. The difference between the two positions constitutes an ongoing debate.

One of the ways that noncloistered men and women came into the presence of the Holy was through PILGRIMAGES. Ever since Constantine's mother **Helena** did a pilgrimage to the Holy Lands in the fourth century, others had followed her to "walk where Jesus walked" and pray where he had prayed. This was true all through the Middle Ages. On such journeys there were moments of ecstasy and ILLUMINATION, as when pilgrims sensed that the Spirit was with them. From the start of pilgrimages, Jerusalem was always the preferred destination, but other holy places became popular too: Rome, Santiago de Compostela in Spain, and Canterbury in England (as the *Canterbury Tales* remind us). Pilgrims went to shrines that had relics, meaning, usually, bones of a saint. Mark's bones, for example, were said to be in the cathedral of Venice. Sometimes pilgrims came home with relics, such as wood from Jesus' cross (there being enough in Europe to build a battleship) or milk from the Virgin Mary's breast. Such seems naive to us now, yet HOLY THINGS—a book, icon, crucifix, flower, crystal—can be of help in "opening to the Spirit."

Talk of pilgrimages and relics reminds us that Christians of the Middle Ages, in both East and West, still had much in common. This included creeds based on decisions by at least seven ecumenical councils. And yet disunity grew between Orthodoxy and Catholicism. One difference had to do with the Holy Spirit in the creeds. In 589 a council (not of the whole church) in Toledo, Spain, added to the Nicene Creed a little phrase that said the Spirit proceeds not just "from the Father" but "from the Father and the Son." The Western emperor liked this *filioque* ("and the Son") clause, which was soon widely adopted. The more conservative Orthodox, however, were appalled on hearing the change, and it became a point of major contention. Greek-speaking East with Byzantine emperor and Orthodox patriarch, and Latin-speaking West, with Frankish king and Catholic pope, drifted apart. In the year 1054 CE "curses" were exchanged between Constantinople and Rome. The two major branches of the Christian faith went separate ways.

Both branches, though, were still reaching out to wider worlds. At Pentecost, centuries before, the Spirit had directed Christians to go into all the world. Now the Spirit seemed to say, "Keep moving." In the year 988 Orthodox missionaries introduced the faith to the Russian people in Kiev. In the previous century, French monks opened up Denmark and began the conversion of Scandinavians (a.k.a. the Vikings!). Conversion of the Norse also proved to be a "local mission project," in that the Danes and others came plundering south and eventually settled in Normandy, Britain, Sicily, and elsewhere—where local Christians could "go to work on them." The Norse responded positively, so that in 1066 at the Battle of Hastings, when the Norman-Vikings defeated the Danish-Vikings (who ruled Saxon England), William the Conqueror began to rule there as a *Christian* monarch.

As the first millennium CE ended, there were few non-Christian kings, lands, or people in Europe. Southern Spain (where Islamic Moors ruled) notwithstanding, Europe was a decidedly Christian continent, Orthodox in the East, Catholic in the West.

High Christendom Years (1100–1450 CE)

Though the two main branches of Christianity split, the Eastern emperor still asked the Western pope to help him fight off Seljuk Turk (and, therefore, Islamic) advances into Byzantine territory. The pope responded positively, broadening the focus to include the Holy Lands and calling for a holy war against "the infidels." Thus Western European armies "of Christ" moved to fight Muslims (Turk, Syrian, and, later, Egyptian). The Crusades went on, roughly, from 1100 to 1300.

There was not much about the Crusades that was "of Christ," but Western Christendom and culture got fall-out benefits by being exposed to the science and culture of Byzantium and Islamic societies. Much of the learning from the Muslims happened via the Moors in Spain, where a crusade against them put Toledo in Christian hands. Then the great Islamic libraries were opened to inquiring Christian eyes. Among the tomes were those of the Greek philosopher Aristotle, who had been lost to the West for more than a thousand years. Aristotle was mined by the greatest theologian and mystic of the late Middle Ages, **Thomas**

Aquinas. Aquinas produced a synthesis of Aristotelianism with Christianity that, though condemned at first, was officially adopted by Catholic bishops in the sixteenth century. Though Aquinas *wrote* much about God, he quit writing during the last years of his life. He went into SILENCE, that being for him the most satisfying way to know the One whom he had called Prime Mover of all things.

Aquinas is but one of many who deepened into God in mystical ways. There were others, women as well as men, who were with the Spirit in the later Middle Ages. Historian and theologian Evelyn Underhill says that there have been three great eras of Christian mysticism: the third, fourteenth, and seventeenth centuries. She says that the fourteenth is "the classic moment for the spiritual history of our race."[2] The following is a list of persons whose mystical spirituality informs us still:[3]

Anselm of Canterbury (1033–1109)
Bernard of Clairvaux (1090–1153)
Hildegard of Bingen (1098–1179)
Joachim of Fiore (1135–1202)
Richard of St.-Victor (d. 1173)
Elizabeth of Schonau (1138–65)
Gertrude the Great (1256–1302)
Dominic (1174–1221), founder of the Order of Friars Preachers
Francis of Assisi (1182–1226), founder of the Order of Little Brothers
Blessed Angela of Foligno (1248–1309)
Bonaventure (1217–74)
Dante Alighieri (1265–1321), author of *Divine Comedy*
Unknown author, *The Mirror of Simple Souls* (ca. 1300)
Meister Eckhart (1260–1328)
John Tauler (1300–1361)
Henry Suso (1295–1366)
John Ruysbroeck (1293–1381)
Thomas à Kempis (1380–1471), author of *Imitation of Christ*
Nicholas of Cusa (1401–64)
Denis the Carthusian (1402–71)
Richard Rolle of Hampole (1300–1349)
Unknown author, *The Cloud of Unknowing* (late 1300s)
Julian of Norwich (1342–1416), author of *Showings of Divine Love*
Bridget of Sweden (1303–73)
Catherine of Siena (1347–80)
Catherine of Genoa (1447–1510), quoted on page 115

This list could be longer, but it includes many persons quoted in the literature, commendable spiritual guides.

Of tremendous inspiration to the Christian life were the writings from this period. **Dante's** *Divine Comedy*, a story of the soul's journey, is one of the enduring contributions to Western literature. While the description of hell is its most read section, the book also has sublime vision of the Absolute. **Thomas à Kempis's** *Imitation of Christ* is the most widely read religious piece—other than the Bible—in the West. *The Cloud of Unknowing* has been "first reading" in contemporary culture as an introduction to CENTERING PRAYER. **Hildegard of Bingen**, among the German mystics, wrote insightfully about the Holy Spirit, saying,

> The Holy Spirit is life that gives life
> Moving all things.
> It is the root of every creature,
> And purifier of all things,
> Wiping away sins,
> Anointing wounds.
> It is radiant life, worthy of praise,
> Awakening and enlivening all things.[4]

To identify a clear sign of the Spirit's purifying presence among people, surely Francis's and Dominic's orders of brothers must be considered. The brothers brought the faith out of the cloisters and closer to the people by their preaching and serving. **Francis of Assisi** introduced a new appreciation for NATURE in his thought and life, which has been helpful in recent creation spirituality. **Dominic** and his Order of Preachers delivered THE WORD with spirit-moving power. He is also reported, probably wrongly, to have begun use of the rosary, which has been a great spiritual aid to millions of the faithful.

While a place for the Spirit was developing in the West, there also was vitality in Eastern Orthodoxy. Hesychasm, propagated by the monks of Mount Athos in the fourteenth century, was something of a new system of mysticism. By a series of practices, involving quiet of body and mind, Hesychasm sought to arrive at the VISION OF THE UNCREATED LIGHT, of God. This would not be the light of God's *essence*, which is unapproachable, the Hesychasts said, but of God's *energy*. Such interpretation is different from the thought of some Western mystics that communion with God in God's self was indeed possible. Hesychasm prescribed breathing exercises, the pressing of the chin against the chest in prayers, letting the mind go into the heart, and the unceasing repetition of what is known as the Jesus Prayer:

Lord Jesus Christ, Son of God, have mercy on me a sinner.

In a later century, according to the book *Way of the Pilgrim*, a Russian Orthodox staretz (holy man) repeated the Jesus Prayer "without ceasing" on a thousand-mile pilgrimage across Russia!

Generally speaking, Christianity was spiritually deeper in this period than almost ever before. For a while, it was strong organizationally too. Pope **Innocent III**, who died in 1216, exercised authority equal to kings. He and later popes controlled a church that began to understand itself in terms of a sacramental system. At the heart of that system were BAPTISM and HOLY COMMUNION, which were always understood as under the direction of the Holy Spirit. So persons baptized into Christ were initiated into the church by water *and the Holy Spirit*. When the faithful gathered at table to receive the bread and wine of Communion (though the cup was withheld from laity), they understood that the elements were changed into the body and blood of Christ *by the action of the Holy Spirit*. How that was so, the church said, was part of the MYSTERY OF THE MASS. Large quantities of ink—and blood—would be spilled in trying to explain this mystery.

Insofar as the sacramental system was thought to work mechanically, it lost much of its spiritual dimension and moved quite far from religion of the heart—or even the mind. If it became a matter of formal physical action, such as a bishop cursorily laying his hand on a confirmand or a priest pronouncing a rote penance, that would be a loss of spirit. And if people began to think that the system operated not by mystery but by magic, that too was a loss. For example, people feared that if a child was not baptized or an elder not given chrism oil at death, he or she was consigned to limbo or worse. Such things did happen, and they represent negative dimensions of the Catholic Church in the late Middle Ages. The Spirit was kept alive in the Jesus-like simplicity of men and women who followed Francis, but not so well in ornate bishops' palaces or richly appointed rooms of the personal chaplains of dukes and duchesses.

Chapter Twelve

The Holy Spirit in the Later Church

Reformations/New Worlds Era (1450–1650 CE)

Franciscans and Dominicans had worked to bear better witness to Christ. So had the Albigenses in France, the Wycliffites in England, the Waldensians in Italy, and the Hussites in Bohemia in the fourteenth and fifteenth centuries. The latter groups' efforts, however, were condemned as heretical and put down by the sword and the fiery stake. In the early sixteenth century in Germany, though, there arose a bear of a thinker and religious spirit, **Martin Luther** of Wittenberg. He would succeed with reform effort where others had failed. As an Augustinian monk and biblical scholar, Luther sought access to God in ways other than through the hierarchy of the church alone (sacramental system). He focused upon what Augustine and Paul before him had regarded as the sine qua non of Christianity: FAITH, faith alone, *sola fides*. Faith functioned for Luther as love functioned for mystics, permitting believers to know they were saved and enabled to enter into holy union. Rudolf Otto says that faith, for Luther, enabled the believer to be "kneaded into one cake with God."[1]

Luther and Lutherans rejected monasticism as not the best expression of Christianity. They also deemphasized the role of Mary and rejected the thought that clergy were somehow closer to God than the laity. Monasticism, veneration of Mary, and set-apart clergy seemed *not* allowed by Scripture, which was immensely important in what came to be called Protestantism. Protestants protested *against* "popes and councils" and *for* the Bible. Scripture, for Luther, came to be used in a wonderful spiritual way in his FOUR-STRANDED GARLAND OF PRAYER. It functioned like *lectio divina*, here with five readings of a text, by which the faithful (1) heard the words, (2) gained instruction, (3) were inspired to give thanks, (4) were led to confession of sin, and (5) opened to letting God be present to them in a word, phrase, image, or feeling.

Joining Luther in theological reformation were **Ulrich Zwingli, John Calvin,** and **John Knox.** They constituted a core for what became the Reformed or Presbyterian tradition. Anglicanism or Episcopalianism came into being by the machinations of King **Henry VIII,** who pulled the church in England away from Rome. He kept the Roman liturgy but had the Latin mass said in English. Henry also dismantled the monasteries, confiscating buildings and properties.

To the three major branches of Protestantism (Lutheran, Reformed, and Anglican) a fourth should be added: the Anabaptist Movement. It actually may have done the most to keep the Spirit alive. Anabaptists advocated and practiced *believers'* baptism, for which the adult baptized needed to be more "Spirit-led." Anabaptist subgroups picked up on notions of God the Holy Spirit at work within believers' hearts.

Two other groups worth mentioning are the Moravians (more below) and the Quakers, proponents of the notion of a divine spark, or the LIGHT OF GOD INDWELLING, in each person. Such light, Quakers believed, was to be cultivated in prayer and quiet. **George** and **Margaret Fox** in England in the late seventeenth century were two of strong Quaker persuasion.

The Protestant Reformation brought on the political and religious breakup of western Europe. Understandably, Protestantism was resisted by popes in Rome and the Spanish kings. So Italian and Spanish—and, later, Hungarian and French—Catholics put together a Counter-Reformation. Reform was instituted through the Council of Trent, which concluded in 1563. It corrected abuses, clarified doctrine, and attempted to win back defectors. In addition, the Roman Church hoped to extend its witness abroad through a new order of zealous missionaries called the Society of Jesus or, simply, the Jesuits. The Jesuits' founder was **Ignatius Loyola,** who gave the world a piece called *Spiritual Exercises*, a book of tremendous religious importance for hundreds of thousands through the centuries.

Within both Catholicism and Orthodoxy, monasteries and convents continued to function. New names became part of the long-running thread of mystics. There were **Teresa of Avila** and **John of the Cross** of the Carmelite Order in Spain during the late sixteenth century. Teresa's contribution to the mystical library is *Interior Castles*; John's is *Dark Night of the Soul*. The latter title and concept was added to the mystic stages of faith, to include

awakening
purification/purgation
illumination
dark night of the soul
union/unitive state

Their insights brought LOVE (verging on erotic love) of God and humanity for each other to highest status.

Mention should be made, too, of **Brother Lawrence,** who wrote *The Practice of the Presence of God.* His little piece of the seventeenth century, now a classic and still being reprinted, presented the idea of knowing or experiencing the HOLY IN ORDINARY LIFE. Brother Lawrence commended "mindfulness" of the nearness of God to people—in the kitchen as much as the chapel.

What was happening in western Europe *internally*, as dramatic as it was, would be dwarfed by what happened *globally*. With improved sea navigation and interest in exploration, the frontiers of the known universe expanded. New Worlds, both west to the Americas and south and east to Africa and Asia, were mapped. With such awareness, the ancient SPIRIT OF PENTECOST reappeared. The missionary impulse was rekindled, first by Catholics, and considerably later by Protestants. In the 1500s, the Catholic Jesuit **Francis Xavier** went as far east as Japan. To the west, Spanish conquistadors went looking for gold, accompanied by Franciscans and Dominicans looking for souls to save. Similarly in northern America, Jesuits accompanied French explorers and trappers into the continent, working with Native people. Not all evangelism, sad to admit, was graciously Christlike, nor was the bringing of black slaves from Africa something of which Christian people could be proud, but over time many Native Americans and Africans joined the faith and added new spiritual vitality, as Indian dance and African American singing bear witness.

The Ecumenical Age (1650 CE–Present)

Protestants got into the Spirit's swing of missionary work in the eighteenth and nineteenth centuries. Missionaries went throughout the world from Europe and, later, from the United States. Moravians inspired by Protestant Count **Nikolaus von Zinzendorf** started work among slaves in the West Indies. Zinzendorf and his Moravian tradition emphasized RELIGION OF THE HEART. Moravians greatly influenced a young Anglican preacher named **John Wesley,** who was on board a ship with them returning from America. Their prayers and singing opened Wesley to the Spirit. That opening, in time, created Methodism, a denomination also "of the heart."

English Methodism and Moravianism were part of PIETISM, a larger rebirth-of-the-Spirit movement that started in the late seventeenth century and extended well beyond the eighteenth. Some say it began after Luther's contributions hardened into rationalistic Lutheranism. Pietism cultivated the inner life under the Holy Spirit, seeking a simple harmony with God and rightness of living. It influenced Protestantism widely and stayed in the Methodist stream of denominations to birth Pentecostalism in recent centuries. What was going on was the opening of the door to the Spirit as a new way of knowing the holy God. Nineteenth-century theologian **Friedrich Schleiermacher** would describe religion as "the *FEELING* of absolute dependence on God."

Room was being made for emotion as never before. In New England, to which many Protestants from old England had come, there arose in the mid-eighteenth century a theologian/scientist/preacher of the first order, **Jonathan Edwards**. Along with **George Whitefield**, Edwards led a Great Awakening (revival), which allowed greater freedom of the will in religious decisions and expression. Edwards spoke, then, of the religious AFFECTIONS, which he believed were enlivened by the Holy Spirit in "new birth." Nineteenth- and twentieth-century evangelists would encourage greater place for the affections—even outright emotionalism—in religious decision making and spiritual life.

In the new United States of America, the Constitution's Bill of Rights (1789) established for the first time a separation of church and state. This meant there would be no state-supported national religion, and church support by individual states soon disappeared also. Suddenly these Protestants realized that they would need to recruit and convert people to their various faith communities if they were to survive.

If the political situation in America was different, so was the cultural climate of the Western world. The late 1600s opened the Age of Reason, and science was also in the air. What was real, rationalists and scientists said, was nature, the material, the physical. The social environment created by these modern, nonspiritual people rejected anything that looked as if it had been handed down by revelation or contained nonrational elements. A general disdain of the "superstitious"—whether it was part of Christianity, Judaism, or some other religion—was held by many. Schleiermacher called such folk "despisers of religion." The historic Christian church was their prime despisee. The despisers thought religion would "fade away" as Education, Science, and Reason (all spelled with capital letters) took over. Metaphysics—consideration of anything beyond the physical—and spirituality (especially anything related to the third person in the Trinity) were thought to have no place in the modern world.

The Spirit did, though, find a place . . . or so it seems. At the start of the nineteenth century, it is estimated that 5 percent of the population of the new United States was church-affiliated. As the twenty-first century begins, 65 percent of the population is so connected, and in polls 95 percent of the citizenry affirm belief in God. In a two-hundred-year period there was a dramatic turnaround. Why? Perhaps the sterility of reason alone or science's inability to fulfill its large promises was their own undoing. Certainly two world wars—led by the best educated, most scientifically and technologically advanced peoples of the world—caused many to question the rationalist and materialist assumptions of modernity. Or maybe it was because the Spirit was at work where the Spirit works best: with INTUITION, FEELING, and the HEART. As Blaise Pascal said, "The heart has reasons that reason knows not of." The domain of religion shifted away from the head and toward the gut. Søren Kierkegaard said it well: religion has to do with SUBJECTIVITY. If God is somewhere, it is at the center of one's inner being (near the will), not in the head or "out there" (for scientists to discover) or "up there" (as in heaven) anymore. This interior orientation is, of course, what the Christian mystics had long held.

Mainline and Evangelical Protestants, Catholics, Jews, and other religionists in America, then, relied more on finding emotional connection and explanation for God. They had to help people say, "I *feel* God's presence," more than depend on revelation (the Bible), tradition (faith history), reason ("proofs" of God's existence), or authority (church hierarchy) to speak of and for God. Conversion and conviction through revivals were much used and quite important, as in the Second Great Awakening in the early 1800s. Evangelical Protestants of the late twentieth century certainly used emotional suasion to enhance their numbers, but all churches generally worked to hold people by heartstrings, employing relevant worship services, good pastoring, appeals to ethnicity, community life, music, support groups, and whatever other means help. The net effect was to attract and hold people.

The faith constituency going the furthest with appeal to Spirit and emotion were charismatic or pentecostal Christians. This group sprang to life in 1907 with the Azusa Street revival in Los Angeles, which historian Robert Owens calls "the greatest religious event of the twentieth century."[2] Pentecostalism grew through the century, encouraging people to express themselves verbally (speaking in tongues) and physically (raising hands and dancing in worship). They were not so much "propositionalists" (requiring assent to certain religious truths, as were other fundamentalist Christians), nor were they overly obsessed with moral dos and don'ts. They were exceedingly open to women and capitalized on ecstasy-friendly praise music. Many Pentecostals have also reengaged in faith healing.

More traditional Christians may find much about this movement objectionable, but it needs to be considered a major way that the Spirit of God has been at work in the last century. Millions of adherents have been brought to Christian faith by this movement, especially in Latin America and Africa. In terms of sheer numbers, Pentecostalism may now be the fourth major branch of Christianity in the world, exceeded only by Orthodoxy, Catholicism, and Protestantism. Time will tell how extensive and enduring the movement is. Church historians Nystrom and Nystrom say, "[T]he explosive growth of Christianity in the non-western world emerged as perhaps the most important development for Christianity in the twentieth century."[3]

What we do not want to miss in the presence of this big, new phenomenon (Pentecostalism) are the evidences of other Spirit-directed things and movements across the Christian spectrum:

- Eastern Orthodoxy's supreme patriarch still intones the Spirit's presence in the Hagia Sophia of Istanbul-not-Constantinople, even though that cathedral is squared by Muslim minarets.
- Other ancient expressions of Christianity continue in the Middle East, though they too have been dominated since the seventh century CE by Islam's strong presence. Still, by the Spirit's tenacity, Syrian and Egyptian Coptic Christianity keeps on keeping on. So do Armenian and Chaldean Christians. There are Aramaic Christians who still speak in the same tongue our Lord used!
- In Russia a major story of survival by the Spirit's grace can be told: Orthodoxy, under communism for almost a century, survived. Thousands of priests and monks were murdered and thousands of churches destroyed, but religion did not "fade away." Russian Orthodox leaders now say reemergence was possible because they kept themselves grounded in the Mystery of the Eucharist. Today holy men and women walk the steppes of Russia chanting the Jesus Prayer "without ceasing."
- Liberation movements have broken forth. Third-world Christians,

black Americans, folks in South Africa, women, and other minorities have moved with winds of change. Christians struggle for the integrity of creation, justice, and peace. The suggestion is that the Spirit is still at work in the world, "blowing in the wind."

- There is certainly spiritual exuberance in the black gospel tradition of singing and preaching, and it has a different texture from that of pentecostal enthusiasm.
- Western Catholic and Protestant men and women go on spiritual life retreats for discernment and deepening. Spiritual direction is undertaken not just by clergy, but also by laity. Centering prayer à la Dionysius the Pseudo-Areopagite and *The Cloud of Unknowing* goes on across denominational lines. Labyrinth walking happens in Episcopal cathedrals and on Southern Baptist church lawns.

It would seem that the Spirit is alive and well in many ways!

Three persons, two of them Catholic, one of them a Protestant, stand out as contemporary leaders in renewed Christian spirituality. One is the Trappist monk and author, **Thomas Merton,** who was an effective advocate for practical mysticism. He said, for example, that

> contemplative Prayer is not so much a way to find God, as a way of resting in him whom we have found, who loves us, who is near to us, who comes to us to draw us to himself.[4]

A younger colleague of Merton's was Father **Henri Nouwen,** who has played a major role in introducing both clergy and laity to the contemplative life. His book *The Wounded Healer* has been an inspiration for Protestant and Catholic clergy alike. Finally, Protestant **John Mogabgab** should be mentioned. He edits the United Methodist publication *Weaving: A Journal of the Christian Spiritual Life,* which has been a deep spiritual source for many.

All of this suggests that there is considerable crossover between historically separated traditions. In the past century, there has been a coming together of Christian believers ecumenically. A few denominations have merged their separate identities, while many others are in partnering conversation, and all give lip service, at least, to the restoration of the oneness of Christ's body. A sign of the Holy Spirit's involvement in the ecumenical movement is found in the World Council of Churches primary symbol: a boat (symbol of the church) riding on the waves of the world, with a cross as its mast and a sweeping line coming from one arm of the cross to the foot, suggesting a sail. That sail reminds us that the boat is propelled yet by the wind—*ruach*—Spirit who brooded over the waters at creation.

Conclusion to Part 4

Six practices historically have made up the core of the Christian spiritual tradition. They are, in Latin and English:

> *lectio*—READING
> *meditatio*—MEDITATION
> *oratio*—PRAYER
> *contemplatio*—CONTEMPLATION
> *visio*—SEEING
> *conjunctio*—UNION

These we have seen appearing in the four-thousand-year story of the Christian faith. The patriarchs and matriarchs of ancient Israel, Jesus with Martha and Mary, abbas and abbesses in the desert, cloistered monks and nuns, brothers and sisters beneath the stars, reformers and counter-reformers, peasants and poets, counts and dishwashers are all part of the many faithful who have been led by the Spirit. Often they have gone inward and been illumined beyond sense and thought by the One who is W/HOLY OTHER and yet NEARER THAN BREATH.

Discussion Questions for Part 4: The Holy Spirit

1. When people say, "I'm not religious, but spiritual," what do they mean? How, if at all, is this spirituality different from Christian spirituality?

2. Recount the many ways in which the Spirit is mentioned in the Bible. Do some ways seem more authentic than others? Which?

3. In the development of Christian doctrine through the centuries, the Holy Spirit seems to have received short shrift. Why? Is there something difficult about the Spirit that makes it hard to say much?

4. Is this, as the author suggests, the age of the Spirit? What evidence suggests it is? What evidence suggests it is not? Where are you and your church in this age?

Notes

Part 1: Central Historical Events

1. H. Richard Niebuhr, *The Responsible Self: An Essay on Christian Moral Philosophy* (New York: Harper & Row, 1963), 25 and 126.

Chapter 1: Biblical Times

1. Other than the Bible itself, there is little—so far, *no*—archaeological evidence of this event's occurrence. What can be said with certainty is that the "centrality of the event in the early poetry indicates the likelihood of some antecedent historical event involving a redeemed Israelite group and a disaster upon an Egyptian force at some body of water, but reconstruction beyond these limits is precarious" (*Anchor Bible Dictionary*, ed. David Noel Freedman [New York: Doubleday, 1992], 6:621).
2. Notes from class taught by B. Davie Napier, Yale Divinity School, 1960.
3. René Girard builds, essentially, a unified field theory (for understanding history, literature, culture, politics, etc.) around the death and resurrection of Christ. See his thought in Gil Bailie, *Violence Unveiled: Humanity at the Crossroads* (New York: Crossroad Publishing Co., 1999), 4–7 and 217.

Chapter 3: The Later Church

1. Kenneth Scott Latourette, *A History of Christianity* (New York: Harper & Brothers, 1953), 1063.

Part 2: God

1. Karen Armstrong, *A History of God: The 4000-Year Quest of Judaism, Christianity and Islam* (New York: Ballantine Books, 1993), xx.
2. Elizabeth A. Johnson, *She Who Is: The Mystery of God in Feminist Theological Discourse* (New York: Crossroad Publishing Co., 2001), 65.

Chapter 5: God in the Early Church

1. A quite good treatment of these theological subtleties may be found in Karen Armstrong's *A History of God*, 69, 116, and 254.

2. Quoted in James C. Howell, *Exploring Christianity: The Bible, Faith, and Life* (Harrisburg, PA: Trinity Press International, 2001), 125.

Chapter 7: Jesus in Biblical Times

1. Johnson, *She Who Is: The Mystery of God in Feminist Theological Discourse*, 95.
2. *Jesus at 2000*, ed. Marcus Borg (Boulder, CO: Westview Press, 1997), 10; and Paula Fredriksen, *From Jesus to Christ: The Origins of the New Testament Images of Jesus* (New Haven, CT: Yale University Press, 1988), 127–30.
3. John Shelby Spong, speaking at First Congregational United Church of Christ, Colorado Springs, CO, October 24, 2004.
4. Stephen Neill, *Jesus through Many Eyes: Introduction to the Theology of the New Testament* (Philadelphia: Fortress Press, 1976), 16 and 45.

Chapter 8: Jesus in the Early Church

1. Jaroslav Pelikan, *Jesus through the Centuries: His Place in the History of Culture* (New Haven, CT: Yale University Press, 1985), 122.

Chapter 9: Jesus in the Later Church

1. Pelikan, *Jesus*, 158.
2. Quoted from a speech by Marcus Borg at Colorado College in Colorado Springs, CO, April 6, 2002. The same phrase is used in his edited book, *Jesus at 2000*.
3. Borg, *Jesus at 2000*, 10 and 11; Borg, *Jesus at 2000*, 11; and Marcus J. Borg, *Meeting Jesus Again for the First Time: The Historical Jesus and the Heart of Contemporary Faith* (San Francisco: HarperCollins, 1994), 30.
4. Neill, *Jesus through Many Eyes*, 2–3.

Part 4: The Holy Spirit

1. Rudolf Otto, *The Idea of the Holy* (New York: Oxford University Press, 1958), 38.
2. Robert N. Bellah and others, *Habits of the Heart: Individualism and Commitment in American Life* (New York: Harper & Row, 1985), 221.
3. Sean P. Kealy, "Holy Spirit," in *Eerdmans Dictionary of the Bible*, ed. David Noel Freedman (Grand Rapids: Wm. B. Eerdmans Publishing Co., 2000), 601.

Chapter 10: The Holy Spirit in Biblical Times

1. Otto, *The Idea of the Holy*, 5 and 51.
2. Borg, *Jesus at 2000*, 11.
3. Charles Williams, *The Descent of the Dove: A Short History of the Holy Spirit in the Church* (Vancouver, BC: Regent College Publishing, 1997), 162.
4. Harry Emerson Fosdick, *A Guide to Understanding the Bible: The Development of Ideas within the Old and New Testaments* (New York: Harper & Brothers, 1938), 231.

Chapter 11: The Holy Spirit in the Early Church

1. Williams, *Descent of the Dove*, 28.
2. Evelyn Underhill, *Mysticism: The Preeminent Study in the Nature and Development of Spiritual Consciousness* (New York: Doubleday, 1990), 454. On 461, she calls the fourteenth century "the Golden Age of Mysticism."
3. Underhill, *Mysticism*, Appendix, "Historical Sketch of European Mysticism ...," 453–73.

4. *Hildegard of Bingen: Mystical Writings*, ed. Fiona Bowie and Oliver Davies (New York: Crossroad, 1990), 118.

Chapter 12: The Holy Spirit in the Later Church

1. Otto, *Idea of the Holy*, 205.
2. Noted in promotion piece for Robert R. Owens, *Speak to the Rock: The Azusa Street Revival, Its Roots and Its Message* (Lanham, MD: Rowman & Littlefield Publishing Group, 2003).
3. Bradley P. Nystrom and David P. Nystrom, *The History of Christianity: An Introduction* (New York: McGraw-Hill, 2004), 378.
4. Quoted in Richard J. Foster, *Streams of Living Water: Celebrating the Great Traditions of Christian Faith* (San Francisco: HarperSanFrancisco, 1998), 344.

Glossary

abba, abbess. Head of a religious order of men (also called an **abbot**) or of women (also called a **prioress**).

advent. "Coming." With a capital A, it suggests the season before Christmas.

Adventism. The nineteenth-century movement that expected the second coming of Christ.

Anabaptist. Branch of the Protestant church *against* the baptism of children but *for* the baptism of believing adults.

Anglican. Related to the Church of England, the church known in America as the Episcopal Church.

apocalypse. The revelation of the "last things."

apocalyptic. Related to "end times."

Apocrypha. Loose collection of books considered sacred and included in the Bible of some Jewish and Christian groups; written in the intertestamental or Second Temple Period; considered deuterocanonical (secondary canon).

apologist. One who explained or worked to defend the faith and make it acceptable to others.

apostles. The twelve closest disciples of Jesus, all thought to have gone out to found Christian churches in the world.

archbishop. A bishop of the highest rank who supervises other bishops.

ascension. Newer Testament says Jesus "ascended," went up into heaven, forty days after his resurrection; so there is an ascension day celebrated in the church. Catholic tradition says Mary also ascended.

asceticism. Denial of the body for purposes of spiritual growth.

baptism. A sacrament of the church using water, by which one enters the church.

Baptist. That branch of the Protestant church that practices believers' baptism by immersion.

Basileia. Usually "of God," meaning God's kingdom, kingly realm/reign/rule, sovereignty, dominion, empire, monarchy, domination-free order.

Byzantium. Site of modern Istanbul, formerly Constantinople; term also refers to Byzantine Empire.

caesaropapism. System where secular ruler has authority over the church, e.g., Byzantine emperor over Orthodox patriarch.

canon. "Ruler" or measuring rod for what are the sacred or approved books of the Bible.

cathedral. Major church, often where a bishop's "chair" (*cathedra*) was; a pronouncement ex cathedra would be something "from on high," the chair of a bishop.

catholic. Universal.

Catholic. Referring to the Western or Roman branch of the Christian church.

charismatic. Pertaining to gifts of the Spirit, such as speaking in tongues.

congregational. A form of church government where individual churches are self-governed.

credo, creed. "I believe" statement of faith adopted by the church to define both religious doctrine and what is heretical; often recited by Christians in worship.

crucifixion. A means of execution by attaching the victim to a cross until death comes; Jesus was executed in this way.

Crusades, the. Military campaigns of eleventh through thirteenth centuries to wrest control of the Holy Lands from the Muslims.

deism. Understanding of distant God who created universe and lets it run by laws of nature.

Diaspora. The dispersion or spread of the Jewish people into the Gentile world, from Persia to Spain, starting in the sixth century BCE.

disciples. The first followers of Jesus, but any who follow a teacher.

dualism. Belief that world is divided between forces of good and evil, God and Satan.

ecclesial. Related to "church."

ecumenical. From *oikoumene* ("whole household," "inhabited world"), now suggesting all the churches together, describing the movement toward Christian unity.

epiphany. Window (pane) into the Holy, a seeing or revelation.

Epiphany. A holy day, the twelfth day after Christmas, celebrating Jesus' being revealed to the Gentile magi.

episcopal. Having to do with a bishop.

Episcopal. A branch of the church in the United States related to the Church of England (Anglican).

eucharist. Meaning "thanks" as in prayer, but also meaning Holy Communion.

evangel. Good news.

Evangelicalism. That branch of the Protestant church especially committed to "soul winning."

evangelism. Work at winning nonbelievers to the faith.

excommunication. Expelling a person from participation in the church.

exodus, the. The thirteenth-century BCE escape/deliverance of the people of Israel from slavery in Egypt.

filioque. Latin meaning "and from the Son," a phrase added to the creeds by the Western church but not accepted by the Orthodox East.

final form. The shape that a book of the Bible (one that might have had several authors over time) finally took in the canon.

friar. Brother in a religious order.

fundamentalism. The conservative theological movement of the twentieth century based on assent to certain basic tenets, such as the inerrancy of Scripture.

Gentiles. Non-Jews in the Newer Testament, usually meaning "Greeks."

God-fearers. Gentiles drawn to Judaism without becoming Jews.

gnostic. One who has special "knowledge" not available to all.

Gnosticism. More spiritual or purely intellectual than incarnational, is usually considered heresy.

gospel. "Good news."

Gospel. A book in the Newer Testament in which the story of Jesus is told: Matthew, Mark, Luke, or John.

henotheism. Belief that there is one god who is stronger than or above other gods.

heretic. One who is not an orthodox believer, but considered in error with regard to matters of doctrine.

Hesychasm. A form of eastern mysticism emphasizing inner quiet and repetitive prayer.

iconoclasm. Destruction of images.

incarnation. Becoming flesh; traditional Christian belief is that Jesus is the incarnation of God, or God in human form.

indulgence. A forgiveness of sin to avoid everlasting punishment. First given to crusaders, they soon were sold by the medieval church.

liturgical. Pertaining to worship.

liturgy. Order of worship with prayers, reading, songs, etc.

Logos. Greek word meaning "Word."

Lutheran. Branch of the Protestant church that followed Martin Luther, originally mostly northern European.

martyr. Literally "witness," one who dies for his or her faith.

Methodism. Protestant denomination founded by John Wesley in eighteenth-century England.

monasticism. Practice of separating from the world and living alone or in community with other **monks** in a monastery; or, if a woman, with other **nuns** in a convent or nunnery.

monotheism. Belief in one God.

mysticism. Religious approach that stresses direct and intuitive experience of God.

neo-orthodoxy. The twentieth-century theological movement emphasizing traditional tenets of the faith, Christ of the creeds as much as Jesus of history.

Newer Testament. This author's preferred designation of the New or Second Testament or "Christian Bible"; this term suggests a time difference from the Older Testament, but not that it somehow supercedes the earlier compiled writing.

Older Testament. This author's preferred designation for the Old or First Testament or "Hebrew Bible"; this term suggests difference from the Newer Testament in time of composition, but not that it is of secondary importance.

orthodox. Right belief or true doctrine.

Orthodox. Referring to the Eastern branch of the church, including the Greek, Russian, Serbian, etc., Orthodox churches.

patriarch. In the Bible a title given to Abraham, Isaac, and others. In church history the title given to bishops of important cities. The Oecumenical Patriarch is in Constantinople/Istanbul.

Pantocrator. "Ruler of all," icon of God the judge, placed on Orthodox church ceilings.

Pentecost. Jewish holy day fifty days after Passover (or Easter), when the Holy Spirit came upon Jesus' followers, birthing the church.

Pentecostalism. A movement in the church emphasizing the Holy Spirit and characterized by ecstatic expression, including speaking in tongues.

Pietism. Movement in Protestantism which emphasizes personal piety and feelings over institutions or doctrines.

polytheism. Belief that there are many gods.

Presbyterian. Reformed Protestant denomination started in Scotland by John Knox in the sixteenth century.

Protestant. One who is not an Orthodox or a Catholic believer, belonging to that branch of the church that "protested" *against* error in Catholicism and was *for* testimony from the Bible about faith matters; **Protestantism** began in the sixteenth century CE in northern Europe.

Psalms, the Psalter. Book of 150 songs in the Older Testament (written by many persons over many years but) attributed to King David as the **Psalmist**.

reformation. The attempt to correct or change church belief or practices; with capital **R**, it refers to the movement of Protestantism that broke from the Roman Church in the sixteenth century; the **Counter-Reformation** was the Catholic attempt to stop the Protestant movement.

Reformed. Referring to the branch of the Protestant church associated with John Calvin and Presbyterian-like beliefs and practices.

relics. Remains, usually bones, of a saint, often venerated, thought to have miraculous power.

resurrection. Restoration into life from death, referring especially to Jesus, but also to all who have died in the Lord.

sacrament. Holy rite, an outward sign of an invisible grace. Catholics have seven sacraments, Protestants two: baptism and Holy Communion.

sanctus. Latin, "holy."

Sanctus, the. "Holy, holy, holy," words from Isaiah 6:3, said or sung in worship, usually at the time of Communion.

see. "Seat" or city where a bishop and an important church may be.

simony. Buying and selling church offices.

Tanakh. Abbreviation for Older Testament with Law, Prophets, and Writings.

theism. Worldview anchored in the belief there is a God.

theophany. An appearance or revelation of a deity.

Theotokos. "God-bearer," a title to honor the Virgin Mary.

Trinity. Christian belief that the one God has been revealed in three "persons"; a **Trinitarian** is a person who holds to this orthodox position.

Vatican. Headquarters of Roman Catholic Church, home of the pope; two all-church councils have been held in the Vatican.

Yahweh. Name of the LORD, once translated as "Jehovah"; a **Yahwist** is a person who worships Yahweh.

Zoroastrianism. A religion of Persia that is dualistic in theology; it influenced Hebrew religion during the Persian Period (539–333 BCE).

For Further Reading

Introduction (Basic Resources)

Anderson, Bernhard W. *The Unfolding Drama of the Bible: Eight Studies Introducing the Bible as a Whole*. Philadelphia: Fortress Press, 1990.

Bainton, Roland H. *The Church of Our Fathers*. New York: Charles Scribner's Sons, 1950.

Bingham, D. Jeffrey. *Pocket History of the Church*. Downers Grove, IL: InterVarsity Press, 2002.

Campbell, Alexander. *The Covenant Story of the Bible*. New York: Pilgrim Press, 1986.

González, Justo L. *Church History: An Essential Guide*. Nashville: Abingdon Press, 1996.

Johnson, George. *Opening the Scriptures: A Journey through the Stories and Symbols of the Bible*. Toronto: United Church Publishing House, 1992.

Marty, Martin E. *A Short History of Christianity*. Philadelphia: Fortress Press, 1987.

Nystrom, Bradley P., and David P. Nystrom. *The History of Christianity: An Introduction*. New York: McGraw-Hill, 2004.

Central Historical Events

Great Events of Bible Times: New Perspectives on the People, Places and History of the Biblical World. Edited by David Goldstein and John Ferguson. Garden City, NY: Doubleday & Co., 1987.

Grenz, Stanley J., David Guretzki, and Cherith Fee Nordling. *Pocket Dictionary of Theological Terms*. Downers Grove, IL: InterVarsity Press, 1999.

Ingpen, Robert, and Philip Wilkinson. *Encyclopedia of Events that Changed the World: Eighty Turning Points in History*. New York: Viking Studio Books, 1991.

Introduction to the History of Christianity. Edited by Tim Dowley. Minneapolis: Fortress Press, 2002.

Marty, Martin E. *The Christian Story*. Videotape issued in 1999 by Tabgha Foundation in Minneapolis.

McBride, Alfred. *The Story of the Church: Peak Moments from Pentecost to the Year 2000*. Cincinnati: St. Anthony Messenger Press, 1983.

"The 100 Most Important Events in Church History." *Church History*, (1990): Vol. IX No. 4.

Time Line

Asimov, Isaac, and Frank White. *The March of the Millennia: A Key to Looking at History.* New York: Walker & Co., 1991. Especially see front and back endpapers.

Bainton, Roland. *The Church of Our Fathers.* New York: Charles Scribner's Sons, 1950. See the inside front and back jacket covers.

Campbell, Alexander. "Chronological Table." In *The Covenant Story of the Bible.* New York: Pilgrim Press, 1986.

Great Events of Bible Times: New Perspectives on the People, Places and History of the Biblical World. Garden City, NY: Doubleday & Co., 1987. Contributors: Bruce M. Metzger, David Goldstein, and John Ferguson.

Hannah, John D. *The Kregel Pictorial Guide to Church History.* London: Angus Hudson Ltd., 2000. Great foldout.

Johnson, George. "A Biblical Timeline." In *Opening the Scriptures: A Journey through the Stories and Symbols of the Bibles.* Toronto: United Church Publishing House, 1992. The simplest schema for the biblical millennia.

Peterson, Susan Lynn. *Timeline Charts of the Western Church.* Grand Rapids: Zondervan Publishing House, 1999. Chronologies by theology, people, cultures, and texts.

Robinson, Thomas. *The Bible Timeline.* Nashville: Thomas Nelson Publishers, 1992. Excellent book, reflecting current scholarship.

"Time Line." In *The HarperCollins Study Bible (New Revised Standard Version)*, xli. New York: HarperCollins, 1993.

The Wall Chart of World History. Drawn by Professor Edward Hull. London: Dorset Press, 1989. Incredible detail in the fine print.

Walton, Robert C. *Chronological and Background Charts of Church History.* Grand Rapids: Academie Books, Zondervan Publishing House, 1986.

God

Armstrong, Karen. *A History of God: The 4000-Year Quest of Judaism, Christianity and Islam.* New York: Ballantine Books, 1993.

González, Justo L., and Zaida Maldonado Perez. *An Introduction to Christian Theology.* Nashville: Abingdon Press, 2003.

Harris, Stephen L. *Understanding the Bible: A Reader's Introduction.* Palo Alto, CA: Mayfield Publishing Co., 1985.

Howell, James C. *Exploring Christianity: The Bible, Faith, and Life.* Harrisburg, PA: Trinity Press International, 2001.

Lohse, Bernard. *A Short History of Christian Doctrine.* Philadelphia: Fortress Press, 1985.

Tanner, Norman P. *The Councils of the Church: A Short History.* New York: Crossroad Publishing Co., 2001.

Urban, Linwood. *A Short History of Christian Thought.* New York: Oxford University Press, 1995.

Jesus

Borg, Marcus J. *Meeting Jesus Again for the First Time: The Historical Jesus and the Heart of Contemporary Faith.* San Francisco: HarperCollins, 1994.

Fredriksen, Paula. *From Jesus to Christ: The Origins of the New Testament Images of Jesus.* New Haven, CT: Yale University Press, 1988.

Jesus at 2000. Edited by Marcus Borg. Boulder, CO: Westview Press, 1997.

Neill, Stephen. *Jesus through Many Eyes: Introduction to the Theology of the New Testament.* Philadelphia: Fortress Press, 1976.

Pelikan, Jaroslav. *Jesus through the Centuries: His Place in the History of Culture.* New Haven, CT: Yale University Press, 1985.

The Holy Spirit

Foster, Richard J. *Streams of Living Water: Celebrating the Great Traditions of Christian Faith* (esp. chapter 2). San Francisco: HarperSanFrancisco, 1998.

Holl, Adolf. *The Left Hand of God: A Biography of the Holy Spirit*, trans. by John Cullen. New York: Doubleday, 1998.

Holmes, Urban T., III. *A History of Christian Spirituality: An Analytical Introduction.* Harrisburg, PA: Morehouse, 2002.

Lane, George A. *Christian Spirituality: A Historical Sketch.* Chicago: Loyola Press, 2004.

Otto, Rudolf. *The Idea of the Holy: An Inquiry into the Non-rational Factor in the Idea of the Divine and Its Relation to the Rational.* Trans. John W. Harvey. New York: Oxford University Press, 1958.

The Story of Christian Spirituality: Two Thousand Years, from East to West. Gordon Mursell, general editor. Minneapolis: Fortress Press, 2002.

Underhill, Evelyn. *Mysticism: The Preeminent Study in the Nature and Development of Spiritual Consciousness.* New York: Doubleday, 1990.

Williams, Charles. *The Descent of the Dove: A Short History of the Holy Spirit in the Church.* First published in 1937; reprint, Vancouver, BC: Regent College Publishing, 1997.

Printed in the United States
93052LV00003B/256-333/A